The Command and the Promise: Reflections on Psalm 119

The Command and the Promise: Reflections on Psalm 119

by
Trudy Pettibone

Dove
Publishers

Dove Christian Publishers
P.O. Box 611
Bladensburg, MD 20710-0611
www.dovechristianpublishers.com
Copyright © 2014 by Trudy Pettibone

ISBN 13: 978-0-9903979-3-9

Printed in the United States of America

Also by Trudy Pettibone

**Together: Devotions for Young
Children and Families**

Table of Contents

INTRODUCTION

This is a devotional book, in two senses. First, I think you might best use it in brief, devotional settings. Secondly, I developed these reflections through my personal devotion time. I first discovered Psalm 119 as a devotional medium several years ago. Each day, I would choose two parts of this alphabet acrostic, and pray through them. The psalm nicely lends itself to prayer because it has all the earmarks of being a prayer. It is addressed to God, and contains praise, petition thanksgiving, and other elements of prayer.

One day, the words of verse 125 "that I may know your teachings" jumped out at me. I grabbed a pad I kept at hand for Bible study and began brainstorming meanings of the word "teachings" and the phrase "to know." That was the first of many such devotional sessions. Sometimes I would focus on individual words, other times the whole verse. Some months ago, I realized that I had compiled a substantial library of notes on this 176-verse prayer. When I had at least one verse under each section, I began collating and comparing the material. This book is the result, and I hope you find my reflections meaningful and helpful.

The psalm consists of twenty-two sections of eight verses each, with a consecutive letter of the Hebrew alphabet beginning each section. The verses of each section have a relationship to other verses in that section, and all are related to the first word of the section. At the end of this manuscript is an appendix of the first Hebrew words of each section and their relationship to the rest of the verses in the section.

The theme of the whole Psalm is the Word of God. "Word" is also described in such ways as Precept, Commandment, Law, Instructions, and Way. Essentially, it is God's Rule, later recorded in what became Scripture. The Psalmist described his interaction with his Deity through his response to the utterance of the Deity as conveyed through prophets and priests.

The Psalmist knew and related to the Law of Moses. We now understand God's commands as being repeated and conveyed by Christ: to love the Lord God with all one's being and to love others as ourselves [Mark 12:30–31]. This great commandment encompasses all of our interactions with God and others.

The Psalmist proclaimed that following this great commandment of God will bring blessing and peace, but not without some struggle. There were times when the Psalmist couldn't sense the presence of God. There were times he felt overwhelmed by his enemies. Through it all, however, he found great comfort in following God's directions, and so it should be in the Christian life. Our life experiences would not be much different from those of the Psalmist.

I have chosen thirty-five verses for focus, and through these verses, we will explore almost the entire psalm. I discuss each focal verse based on a theme under general headings of The Characteristics and Gifts of God, Humanity's Response to God, and finally, Humanity Alone. I refer to other verses dealing with this theme at the end of each section. First, however, we will deal with two dominant themes that are woven through the psalm: the command and the promise.

I
THE COMMAND

Verse 1 gives us the first description of the command: "the law of the Lord." God's law transcends all time and people. While God's people from the time of Moses—and including our Psalmist—had an ever-expanding set of laws encompassing all aspects of life, we need only refer back to the first ten rules given to Moses, the admonitions we call the ten commandments [Exodus 20:3–17]. The first four describe humanity's ideal relationship to God, the last six relate to our relationships with one another. Jesus summed up these requirements even more tersely: love.

Whether we look at this directive as a command, a recommendation, a precept, a law, or just instructive words, the fact that it comes from Christ puts significant weight behind it. These are "red letter words" in more than just an editorial sense. If we have entered into a relationship with Christ by believing in his redemptive work, our lives will be much better for following the words spoken by Christ.

The Psalmist portrayed various results of obeying the Word: protection, life, joy, righteousness, hope, understanding, and victory over evil. We will examine each of these and more in light of their relevance to our Christian life today. God's Word, given through Scripture, is just as potent today as it was for the Psalmist. It is sad that so many people—even those claiming the name of Christ—ignore, deny, or only rarely consider Scripture. It is a literary chest in which we can find new and wonderful treasures each time we open it.

God's command, word, or law is perfect and is contained in Scripture, but this does not make Scripture perfect. Scripture is the word of God, which contains the Word of God. The difference is more than just a capital or lower case letter. God did not speak every word of Scripture. Every word is, however, a message God has provided so that we can be guided in living Kingdom lives, the life those who claim the name of Christ should be living, the life about which Jesus taught. Scripture contains examples of people doing this properly and improperly. The text gives us guidelines and admonitions. There are promises made, kept, and yet to be fulfilled. Words of encouragement and, yes, curses, fill the pages.

All Scripture is profitable for teaching, doctrine, correction, and discipline [1 Timothy 3:16–17]. For me, "all" means both Old and New Testament. When our spiritual forefathers wrote accounts and letters now in the New Testament, the Old Testament was the only Scripture they had. We must include it in any description of Scripture. Scripture is designed to help us be the best we can be as Kingdom citizens. The Psalmist recognized these things, even though his access to texts was limited, if not non-existent. The Psalmist likely lived in a time where God's message was predominantly conveyed in an oral context.

The texts and precepts of Scripture give us a wonderful glimpse into the past, if we can accept them as such. We can't say that because something was true for a certain group of people at a certain time, it is true for us now. An example is the communal way of living in the early church [e.g., Acts 2:42–47]. The people shared all things in common and submitted to regulations about their gathering and participation. Very few groups worship and live like that today. We gather for worship and instruction as we feel free, and it is within our determination as to whether or not we support the group. Does that mean that we are all wrong? Not likely. Let's distinguish between cultural and temporal situations and eternal truths.

We can learn from the Psalmist's desire to be taught the Word, his delight in following God's commands, and his anger at those who deny the law of the Lord. The Psalmist demonstrated faithfulness in his proclamation of the Word—even to kings—and his dependence on the Word, even during suffering. Because of his faithfulness to God's commands, he claimed the right to voice expectations of God, especially in light of the promise which the Lord has made.

II
THE PROMISE

No single word appears in this text as much as the word "promise." The Psalmist's joy, obedience, and expectations were based on the promise which our author claimed. We will look at promises made by the Psalmist, but the more important element is the promise understood and relied upon by the Psalmist. The word "promises" does not appear in this text; the promise is always singular. Never does the Psalmist describe the promise specifically. As we look at the references, however, we might get a glimpse into his understanding.

Many believe that the author of this psalm was David, a young man who went from shepherd to king, who saw sorrow and joy, tribulation and exaltation. The author of 1 Samuel describes him as a man after God's own heart [1 Samuel 13:14; Acts 13:22], even though he was an adulterer and murderer. He never turned away from God, even in the depths of his despair, and would be a perfect candidate for authorship of this psalm.

The Lord made several promises to David, the most relevant of which is the promise that one of his descendants would always sit on the throne of Israel. David descended from Israel's son Judah, and Jesus came from the same line. This is, in fleshly terms, a promise of eternity, and Jesus is a

King for eternity. Eternal reign may be one promise on which the Psalmist relied. If David's family was so special to the Lord that he would make them into an eternal dynasty, why should David not trust in that promise for his day to day existence, provision, and protection? He had a foundation for his faith.

There are also some "generic" promises that the Psalmist may have relied on: God's promise to Israel, set forth in Genesis 28, of continual presence, blessing, and guidance. Joshua undertook the leadership of the Israelites with the Lord's promise that he would never leave him nor forsake him. These are promises that pass through the ages, and through Christ, we can claim them. Therefore the same reliance on promise made by the Psalmist can be ours.

John Ortberg says that God's promise of presence is the most primary promise of Scripture.[1] We can turn our back on God, but when we turn back, God is always there. From the time of Adam, God has been with the people God created. Even though Adam tried to hide, God sought him out. Moses tried to escape in the wilderness, but he couldn't get away from God. A wonderful element of God's presence is that where God is, all that God represents is present.

As we look at the focal verses and their adjuncts, we will also discuss the Psalmist's dependence on promise as it relates to the subject matter.

III
CHARACTERISTICS AND GIFTS OF GOD

1. Understanding — Verse 32:
(I run the way of your commandments,) for you enlarge my understanding. **TEV***: (I will eagerly obey your commands,) because you will give me more understanding. The NIV translates the last part of this verse as: "for you have set my heart free."*

There is some variety in the psalmist's depiction of the result of obedience. "Give me more understanding" and "Enlarge my understanding" sound alike and speak to the Psalmist's desire to know and understand more. The term "set my heart free," at first glance, seems anomalous. We can bring the ideas together with Jesus' words from John 8:32: *and you will know the truth, and the truth will make you free.* Knowing the truth of God's law can indeed free our hearts and increase our understanding.

The Psalmist demonstrated eagerness because he had seen the result of obedience in his life. God's response is the reason for his response; it is why he continued to obey. Obedience brings God's positive response. God honors obedience. All things, including understanding, come from God. The Psalmist looked at this as a very personal thing, and so should we.

God works in our lives individually; someone else's obedience will not bring me understanding. We must obey if we are in Christ. Since we are not perfect, we may sometimes slip, but God looks at the desire of our hearts, at our true intent.

We have to have some understanding of God's ways in order to obey. For the Psalmist, this understanding came from the Law and his response to the Law. Obedience brings greater understanding, and should increase with understanding. The things we do in our lives with which we hope to glorify God will be done more effectively when we have greater understanding. Knowing God better leads to more obedience, which should lead to our becoming brighter lights.

If we love Jesus, we will obey [John 14:15]. As we obey, our understanding of who Jesus is and what he has done will increase. As our understanding increases, we become better able to live and teach others. We should become more obedient. It is a beautiful circle of obedience, blessing, and faith.

Many of us are like Christopher Columbus when it comes to understanding: he didn't know where he was going; he didn't know where he was when he got there; and he didn't know where he had been when he returned. The popular expression is that we "don't have a clue." We sleepwalk through the Christian life, not seeking guidance, not understanding the results of our words and actions, and not really caring. God can't honor that aimless lifestyle. Unfortunately, we will discover when it is too late what the impact of our cluelessness has been. The Lord is willing to provide understanding, and we should do our best to receive.

Understanding or similar ideas are dealt with throughout our Psalm, in verses 27, 34, 73, 99, 100, 104, 125, 130, 144, and 169. The Psalmist requested understanding of God's laws in verse 27, and promised faithful meditation on the laws as a result. The Psalmist repeated this promise in verse 34. In verse 73, the Psalmist based his request for understanding on his own understanding of being created by God. In verse 99, we saw the writer's assertion of more understanding than his teachers and in verse 100, he claimed greater wisdom than the elders. Faithful study of God's Word will indeed take you beyond your natural limitations.

Verse 104 says that the wisdom gained from the Lord's laws caused the Psalmist to hate all bad conduct. The more we learn about the Lord, the more natural it is to want to do right. This Psalmist confirmed his position as the Lord's servant in verse 125. Because of this status, he desired better understanding, so that he may better know his master's desire. We see a New Testament idea set forth in verse 130: explanation of the Lord's teachings brings light and wisdom to those who are untaught.

In verse 144, we see the Psalmist claiming life because of his understanding of the Lord's just and righteous teachings. The Psalmist could claim God's help in verse 169 because of the Lord's promise of understanding.

2. Life — Verse 40:
. . . in your righteousness give me life. **TEV***: . . . give me new life, for you are righteous.*

The Psalmist knew that the righteousness of the Lord brought life to those who would live by it. The idea of "new" is not really in the Greek or Hebrew texts I use, but we are going to look at newness of life in the Christian context, life which comes through the righteousness of Christ. God gives life to all, but new life, eternal life with the Lord, comes through faith and belief in Jesus Christ: 2 Corinthians 5:17: *So if anyone is in Christ, there is a new creation: everything old has passed away; see, everything has become new!* This new life will be an ongoing thing, from the time we first believe until we see Jesus face to face.

Just as we grow and change from childhood through adolescence to adulthood, so we grow and change in our new lives, our Kingdom lives. I am an adolescent in faith, even though I have known Christ for twenty-six years. Starting as babies, drinking the Spiritual milk of the word, we should move on to meatier studies and tasks. What is your life stage of faith at this time?

Too many people never seem to get past the infant stages of Spiritual life. These folks do not participate in the Spiritual disciplines enough to allow these practices to change them. A few Spiritual disciplines are Scripture reading and meditation, personal prayer and worship, fellowship with other believers, and active determination to follow Christ. Some change in our lives is gifted by the Lord, but most of the time, we change because we trust the Lord to help us change and live accordingly. New life in Christ is more than turning over new leaves or following annual resolutions, although these can bring impetus. New life comes from the Lord, who instills in us the Holy Spirit as our guide through our Spiritual journey. It is the Holy Spirit who enables us to grow and change. If we deny the presence or work of the Spirit, how can we ever become all we should be in Christ?

In his parable of the seed [Matthew 13: 1–23; Mark 4:4–8; Luke 8:4–15], Jesus talks about things that stunt our spiritual growth and impair our new life. Moving past the seeds that fall on the path and are eaten by birds, which represent those who never understand or receive, we have the seeds that fall on rocky ground. These receive the message on the surface but it never sinks in. There is no transfer from head to heart. These seedling people stumble when difficulties begin. Things such as rejection by family and friends, requirements for participation in the church, and conflict with other life interests all interfere with growth in the new life, and these people fall away.

The next seeds fall among thorns, which choke and strangle the new life. People represented by these seeds never let spiritual values take precedent over fleshly values. Kingdom values never prevail over earthly. The ways of God cannot gain priority over the things of humanity. These thorn-laden folks might remain in church, passing themselves off as part of God's family, but their lives are barren. Scripture doesn't tell us that these fall away, they just don't bear fruit. Sadly, I think these make up the bulk of people in the church. The world and their flesh have a strong hold on them. These are ecclesiastical bench warmers who may have been in church all their lives, but have never been transformed, have never experienced growth and change and the abundant life that Christ brings.

The new life of God may manifest itself in a number of ways. First, our thoughts will change. We will learn how to bring them into the captivity of obedience to Christ [2 Corinthians 10:5]. We will begin to meditate on things that help us grow in Christ and honor Christ. Thoughts that cause us to consider or engage in things that are not worthy of Christ should be surrendered to Christ. It often amazes me how, when an unwanted thought rears its head, asking Christ to help me take control over it always brings positive results.

Secondly, our attitudes should change. We should see less of the "fleshly" attitudes, such as greed, envy, revenge, self-exaltation, negativity, and more of those attitudes that speak of the Lord's work in our lives. We should experience joy, optimism (not Pollyannaism), and freedom from fear and worry. We should begin to consider others above ourselves, and look first to please the Lord, then others, before ourselves. Patience is important also, because we may not see the fulfillment of these in our lifetimes, but we wait with faith, trusting. The right attitude can affect everything else in our lives, maybe even some things we don't expect. For example, we probably shouldn't be surprised to see better physical and mental health following improved attitudes.

As thoughts and attitudes begin to change, we should see a change in our behavior, both in speech and action. The old things will be less important, replaced by activities which build up and encourage ourselves and others. We should learn to speak the language of faith, using positive expressions instead of speaking defeat and fear. Words and actions which glorify God and build up others should be practiced and practiced, even if we don't feel them. If we are truly committed to God's new life, we can become what we aspire to be.

We can't live God's new life alone. God sent the Spirit to help us, both by guiding us personally and by helping us to understand Scripture. The more we submit to God's control, the more we can enjoy the abundant life Christ came to bring. Practice, determination, and discipline will produce fruit in our new lives.

The Psalmist used the idea of life abundantly in this writing. We see its many forms in verses **37, 50**, 88, 93, 107, 109, 149, 154, 156, 159, and 175. We can look at life as the new life that comes from following God, as preservation from destruction in this world, or as the life which will be lived in eternity with the Lord. It all comes from God.

In verse 88, the Psalmist asked for life so that he may keep the Lord's laws. We see the inverse of this in verse 93, where the writer promised never to neglect the Lord's laws, because they give life. No matter how we look at it, following the Lord's ways and life are irretrievably connected.

The writer spoke of sufferings in verse 107, and we will see this motif again. Because of severe affliction, the Psalmist asked to be kept alive. He was ready to risk his life—holding his life in his hand—for the way of the Lord, according to verse 109. Because of the expectation of the Lord's constant love, the Psalmist asked for mercy and the preservation of life in verse 149. God's compassion is the reason to expect salvation in verse 156, and it is the Lord's steadfast love that brings an expectation for life, according to verse 159.

Verse 154 voices the request that the Lord defend the writer's cause and save him. Usually, it is the Lord's causes that we must defend, but when we are faithful, God will side with us in our endeavors, especially where the unfaithful are involved.

2a. Righteousness — Verse 40:

The Psalmist made a claim to life because of the Lord's righteousness, not his own. Throughout this Psalm, we see this righteousness expressed in two forms: (1) the righteousness of the Lord, and (2) the righteousness of the law and other aspects of the Lord.

(1) Verses 137 and 142 deal with the Lord's righteousness. The Psalmist proclaimed the righteousness of the Lord, and this righteousness is connected with the Lord's justice and truth. These are inseparable.

(2) Verses 7, 62, 106, 123, **138**, 142, 144, 160, and 164 deal with the righteousness of the law. It should be noted that verse 142 appears in both categories. God's righteousness is everlasting, and because of this, God's law can be depended on as being righteous and true. The Psalmist addressed the Lord's righteousness, but he focused on the righteousness of the Lord's commandments.

According to the Psalmist, the Lord is worthy of praise because of the righteousness of the judgments. Verse 62 tells us he awoke in the middle of the night to offer this praise, and in verse 164, we see him offering praise seven times a day.

The Psalmist offered his promise to obey because of the justness of the Lord's instructions in verse 106. In verse 123, we see an expectation of help because of the Lord's righteous promises. The Psalmist knew that all of God's decrees are appointed in righteousness and faithfulness, according to verse 138. The Psalmist extolled the eternal quality of God's edicts in verses 144 and 160.

3. Comfort — Verse 50:

This is my comfort in my distress, that your promise gives me life. **TEV**: *Even in my suffering I was comforted because your promise gave me life.*

Early in my Kingdom walk, I was asked to share a testimony of my faith walk to a Senior Adult class. I talked about how, when I believed in Jesus, the first thing that happened was that I lost a good-paying job. Subsequent financial problems, betrayal by friends, and teenage rebellion made the first years of my Christian walk very difficult. I then shared how I had seen the Lord's hand throughout that time, in meeting financial needs, filling my heart with peace, and changing some of my worst attitudes. It was probably the single biggest period of growth in my new life, filled with struggles, but never without the help and comfort of the Lord.

Following the class, a gentleman approached me and told me that I needed to examine whether or not I was a believer. That really shook me, even though I knew this man's "bed of roses" philosophy about the Christian life. By now, I know that he has faced the Lord and seen the results of Christ's own sufferings. Because Jesus suffered for our sins, does that mean that we won't? I don't find that in Scripture. In fact, we see just the opposite. If we are related to Jesus, we will join him in suffering for his cause.

Not all of our suffering, of course, is for Jesus. One of the reasons I was fired from a good job was because on breaks and lunch—never on the bosses' time—I couldn't help talking about Jesus. Some maturity has helped me time my witness a little better. Many of my other problems, however, were caused by my own bad choices and ignorance. Much of what made those years so difficult were consequences of decisions I had made long before I came to know Christ. Even so, the Lord's comfort was ever present to help me.

Bill and Gloria Gaither used to sing a song that is still heard in my shower, a song called "Through It All." One line in particular speaks volumes: "If I'd never had a problem, I'd never know that God could solve them, I'd never know what faith in God could do." Amen!

During the years of Jesus' walk on earth, he accomplished many things, most importantly the sacrifice of his life for the reconciliation of creation to the Creator, and the subsequent resurrection that guarantees life to those of faith. Before these events, he bestowed wonderful teachings, such as the Sermon on the Mount [Matthew 5]. Some of these are hard for us to hear. He provided examples of how to love and serve others, by feeding 5,000, and washing the feet of his disciples. Not the least important, he suffered through things like the death of a friend, and rejection by his earthly family. Because he experienced such sorrow, he can be a comfort to us in our suffering. That is a great gift!

The Psalmist doesn't always tell us what his distress or suffering might have been. If the Psalmist was David, then Scripture tells us some of the things he suffered. Fear of his life and flight from the jealous King Saul and a highly dysfunctional family are only two examples. No matter what was happening, David was able to bask in the Lord's presence and find peace. Questionable choices, including adultery and murder, did not affect his relationship with the Lord, once repentance was affected.

We don't find a lot about suffering or distress in the rest of the Psalm, but there is more about comfort. The Psalmist took comfort in the Lord's ordinances, according to verse 52. In verse 76, the Psalmist described comfort found in the Lord's love and the promise of that love. The Psalmist looked for the Lord's promise of comfort to come true in verse 82.

4. Fullness of God's Love — Verse 64:

The earth, O LORD, is full of your steadfast love; teach me your statutes. **TEV***: Lord, the earth is full of your constant love. Teach me your commandments.*

When we think about the "earth," in relationship to God, our thoughts should encompass everything, because everything is related to God. Look at all that surrounds you: all nature, people, animals, achievements, structures, activities, and ministry. All these things can show forth the glory of God.

God's steadfast love provides abilities, memories, words, and guidance—through Scripture, the Holy Spirit, and faithful evangelical servants. God provides protection and the provision of all needs and many desires. The manifestations of God's love are countless.

The crowning achievement of God's love is Jesus Christ and that which is given through Christ: salvation, forgiveness, life, peace, comfort, promise, and hope, to name a few. Through the church, the Body of Christ, we have fellowship, ministry, and the opportunity to learn to worship just as we will throughout eternity.

God's love is demonstrated in faithfulness: the sun, moon, and stars and their schedules; the tides; and the seasons, to name a few evident sources. When we look at our calendars, we can trust that scheduled years, months, days, and hours will appear, unless the Lord returns before their arrival. God's love is manifest in the provision of physical needs, friends, jobs, recreation, and loving families. How do you experience the manifestation of God's love?

Although humanity is God's crowning achievement in creation, we see that God also cares for wildflowers, trees, and animals. The love of the Lord is manifest in great beauty in nature. At the time of this writing, I lived in the Adirondacks of New York. I could look out and see part of Gore Mountain, a winter ski destination. Some might find the Adirondack Mountains awesome and inspiring. A few years ago, I was in the Rockies, and they were even more awe-inspiring. I am sure the Alps would be even more so. Wherever we go, we can see wonderful examples of the love and care of God.

Because we see God's love all around us, and because God has placed the love of Christ in our hearts, we should long to know more about God and God's ways. We desire to be more obedient, to want less of ourselves and more of God. We strive to be examples to others of one living in submission to the will of God and under His Lordship.

Once we can see the glory of God in all things, we should desire to be a conduit for God's love, that others might see, hear, and sense God's love in us, and that we might share that love with others. I define love as God's purpose for others flowing through us toward others. Let God show you how to help others see God's love all around them. Seek a heart of obedience, because God has given countless demonstrations of love through countless means. Thank you, Lord.

The Psalmist talked about his life on the earth being ended

by enemies in verse 87, yet he remained faithful to the Lord's command. In verse 90, the Psalmist exalted the faithfulness of the Lord, as demonstrated by putting the earth in place and having it remain. The Psalmist loved the Lord's decrees, according to verse 119, because the Lord treats all the wicked of the earth as dross, not a concept readily associated with Christianity.

The Psalmist asked the Lord to show him how much he was loved in verse 41. In verse 76, our author sought comfort in the Lord's love. The Psalmist sought salvation because of the Lord's love, so that he might keep the Lord's decrees, according to verse 88. The Psalmist asked to be treated according to the Lord's love in verse 124, and expected to be heard because of that love in verse 149. Because the Psalmist loved the Lord's precepts, he expected to have his life preserved, according to verse 159.

5. Punishment/Humbling — Verse 75

I know, O LORD, that your judgments are right, and that in faithfulness you have humbled me. **TEV**: *I know that your judgments are righteous, Lord, and that you punished me because you are faithful.*

The word and idea of punishment is not very popular today. Can we find "acceptable" terms for punishment? We might consider discipline, scolding, or correction. The idea is the same: we have done something wrong. God wants us to do right. God gets our attention, and then works in our lives to help us learn God's ways.

I know that thinking of God as a loving parent is a difficult concept for some who never knew loving parents. Even if our parents were lousy in their parental calling, is it so difficult to understand that God is far above any earthly parent, and fulfills the role of a loving God and parent? I had a wonderful father, so it is easy to relate to God as a loving heavenly father. God, however, is still God and surpasses all expectations and capabilities of earthly parents. As a loving parent, God wants what is best for us. That is why we get correction when we do wrong. Doing right is for my own good, and brings benefits. Doing wrong hurts me—and possibly others—and that is not a good thing.

Many bad things can happen to us in this lifetime. It is not all the correction of God. We can never say that anything we experience is definitely the hand of God. If we are committed to following God, however, we will try to allow everything that happens to us to work for us. This is one of God's most faithful promises: Romans 8:28: *We know that all things work together for good for those who love God, who are called according to his purpose.* Even if what is happening to us is not by God's hand, God can use it for our good, if we allow it.

We have to understand that just because good can come from things, that is not to say that all things that happen are good. Parental abuse and neglect are not in any way "good" things. They are also not the punishment of God for something we have done. Abuse and neglect are evil. The hope and faith we can have is that God can take these evil things and others like them and work in our lives to bring good. One example witnessed in many people: some who have experienced the evil of others have been helped by God to use that horrible experience in their lives to help them help others who might be experiencing the same things. This doesn't make their experience good, but it helps them use their experience for good in the life of others.

What are some of the ways in which we might experience God's discipline? There might be blessings withheld. Maybe we have some rights denied, although as believers, all of our rights are in Christ Jesus. Maybe we enter a time of silence, or a wilderness period, when we don't seem to receive the communication from God to which we had become accustomed. We might experience death or loss—of people, prestige, health, or possessions.

Scripture says that the wages of sin is death [Romans 6:23]. That is not very good grammar, but it is a great theological point. Our part is to properly understand the implications of the word "death." It is not just physical and spiritual death, which is separation from God. Death can come in many forms: the death of a relationship, the death of a dream, of hope, of peace. All of these things can come as the result of disobedience. We don't always recognize some of the changes in our lives as death, but that is often exactly what it is.

How do I, personally, know that I am being chastened by God? I perceive a sense of separation. When I don't please my spouse, I perceive this same sense of separation. I can't really describe it. I just know that things that usually go right start to go wrong. I am used to seeing many blessings in my life, and when I am under God's disciplining hand, I am well aware of the lack of some of those blessings. Think about the ways in which you have seen God's chastening hand.

Let's consider some of the differences between discipline and punishment. Punishment is the cost of doing wrong; discipline is training to do right. Punishment is always to be dreaded, but discipline should be welcomed and appreciated. Punishment brings useless pain, but the pain of discipline is but for a short time, and will bring reward, if we allow it to do its work.

Will God's discipline always have the desired effect? That's up to us. If we continue in doing whatever caused the discipline, we may eventually lose the effect of the discipline, and be left on our own. Our hearts grow cold and calloused, and we reject God's ways. If we respond properly, allowing the discipline to have its way in our lives, the discipline period should soon end, and we will have grown through another stage of our Kingdom life.

God's discipline never means the loss of God's love. It is actually a wonderful sign of God's love, the love of a parent who wants the best for his or her children. There are undoubtedly parents who punish for spite or, even worse, for their own pleasure. God's punishment or discipline is always for our good, and our good is to God's glory.

The Psalmist proclaimed that God punishes because God is faithful. I don't really like the word "punish" for reasons mentioned earlier. In my opinion, when we are speaking about God, "discipline" serves a better purpose. We can't deny, however, that throughout the Old Testament, and into the New, we see examples of God punishing those who refuse to obey.

If God did not care, God would not discipline. We see references to God's "hand," which always refers to the guidance and work of God in our lives. Faithfulness means that God won't step out of character, although that possibility is not ruled out for a God who can do all things. Regardless of what we perceive, God is faithful.

God is as God has always been and will always be. What God once hated, God still hates. What God punished once, God will always punish, although we may not receive or perceive that punishment as immediately as we might see it in Scripture. Even in punishment, however, God's constant love can bring comfort. Romans 5:8 reminds us that Christ died for us, because of God's love, while we were yet sinners.

Through love, grace, and mercy, God has dealt with eternal punishment. God sent his son, Jesus Christ, to receive the punishment we earn by our sin, to die bearing that punishment, and to rise from death so that we can live eternally with him. This act of love is in conflict with much of what we see in God's dealings with the people of the land as God tries to establish a people. That is what God is all about: being God and not human, and we can only trust and obey even though we can't understand.

Because of punishment, the Psalmist had corrected his ways, in verse 67. According to verse 71, punishment helped the Psalmist learn the Lord's commands. In verse 90, the Psalmist knew the eternal duration of the Lord's faithfulness. Our author asserted that God's decrees were appointed in faithfulness in verse **138**.

6. Presence — Verse 98

Your commandment (. . .) is always with me. **TEV**: *Your commandment is with me all the time (. . .).*

In Scripture, we read about reminders of God's commandments, such as the fringe attached to the edge of garments [Numbers 15:39]. The Psalmist was not saying that a reminder of God's commandment was always with him. He said that the commandment itself was with him all the time. He had hidden it in his heart, he could meditate on it at will, and it was at the core of his thought life. So should it be for us.

A couple in the congregation I once served planned to retire together. The man had a few weeks head start, taking the remainder of his vacation time. The day recently came when they could be together all the time. I don't know if their finances permit a lot of travel or other variations from their normal life activities. They will most likely continue a monthly trip to visit a son and new grandson. I think this couple—empty nesters for several years—may find constant presence a bit wearing at times. Few people can abide a constant presence without some resulting strain. I can think of one exception.

The Psalmist said that God's commandment was always with him. Do you picture a shepherd carrying bags of scrolls? Does he have a PDA or laptop with a scripture program? How else could God's commandment be ever with him? The answer is that God was always with him. This is the one Presence with which we can always abide. When God is present with us, all that God represents is with us: God's attributes, God's blessings, and God's commandments.

Think of your computer, loaded with software for tons of applications. Do you ever use all your programs at once? Not likely. I have programs I almost never access, and some I have never used. God with us means all of God with us. We just have to learn to access what is available to us. God's Spirit can help us be obedient to all of God's law, but we have to open that program. We have to make the determination to obey, trust God to help us, and turn away from the temptation to walk in our way. God's commandments are always with us, because God is always with us to help us obey.

In verse **151**, the Psalmist asserted the nearness of the Lord and the truth of the commandments. The commandments are true because God is true. It is very difficult to separate any aspect of God from the being of God. In verse 150, the Psalmist spoke of the nearness of enemies, relationships we can do without, but one in which, like the Psalmist, we can call on God for help.

7. Eternity — Verses 111 and 112

112: Your decrees are my heritage forever . . . . **TEV**: *Your commandments are my eternal possession. . . . 112: I incline my heart to perform your statutes forever, to the end.* **TEV**: *I have decided to obey your laws until the day I die.*

If some aspect of our lives is truly eternal, it does not end when our time in this life ends. After belief in Jesus Christ, obeying God's laws until the day we die will truly grant us life. For the Psalmist, who knew law and not grace, such guarantee could come only by faithfully following God's laws, as given through Moses. Holding God's commandments as an eternal possession means they will always be with us. Even when we see our Lord, God's commandments will still be in effect. We will just experience them in a different way.

Will there be any inclination not to obey God's laws when we are with the Lord? After all, we have stories in Scripture of the rebellion of angels in God's presence [2 Peter 2:4]. Actually, I have a hard time imagining disobedience in heaven. If we have had the faith and accompanying works worthy of life, can you imagine disobeying after we enter the presence of Christ?

In the New Jerusalem, there will not be grief, crying, or pain [Rev. 21:4]. Since these things are often the result of disobedience, I have to believe there will be no disobedience. Also, in Revelation 21:27, we see that impurity, shameful things, or liars will not enter the city. Those whose names are written in the Lamb's book of life will enter, and there will be obedience and life.

John Donne described this eternity beautifully: "I shall rise from the dead, from the prostration . . . of death, and never miss the sun, which shall be put out, for I shall see the Son of God, the Sun of Glory, and shine myself as that sun shines. I shall rise from the grave, and never miss this city, which shall be nowhere, for I shall see the city of God, the New Jerusalem. I shall look up and never wonder when it shall be day, for the angel will tell me that time shall be no more, and I shall see and see cheerfully that last day of judgment, which shall have no night, never end, and be united to the Ancient of Days, to God Himself, who had no morning, never began."[2]

In the **TEV**, the idea of forever seems to extend only to the life of the Psalmist, according to verse 112, so the following verses are all based on the NRS.

In verse 44, the Psalmist promised to keep the law continually, closing with the emphasis of "forever and ever." In verse 112, the Psalmist "inclines his heart" to perform the Lord's statutes "forever, to the end." In the **TEV**, "the end" means the end of his life.

In verse 89, we see no doubt of the author's belief: the Lord exists forever and the Word of the Lord is firmly fixed in heaven. In verse 144, our author declared the righteousness of the decrees forever, and asked for understanding that he might live. The decrees themselves, according to verse 152, declare their own eternal establishment. In verse **160**, the Psalmist attested that the sum of God's Word is truth, and every ordinance endures forever.

8. Protection — Verse 114
You are my hiding place and my shield (. . .). **TEV**: *You are my defender and protector (. . .).*

As a non-Christian, I had some self-destructive tendencies. Looking back, it seems that everything that seemed good in my life had to be damaged in some way. Special recognition brought a desire to turn away from the way recognized. New clothes were quickly marred. Good relationships didn't seem to be something I was worthy of, so faults were inevitably "discovered" and the relationship was ended. Now, as I pray for our family, I pray that the Lord will protect us from the harm that comes from within as well as from outside of us. I really could have used that protection in my youth.

God is our defender and protector. How many times a day does God protect us? The other day I chopped a finger. Did God keep it from being worse? Is God guiding me to care for it so it doesn't become infected? Are there angels who are directing our paths to save us from more harm than we encounter?

I choose the affirmative in each of those questions. Scripture speaks too often of God's protection, and offers enough demonstration of it for us to deny its existence. God's protective power is constantly at work in the lives of believers, in ways both big and small. When I meet the Lord, I envision seeing a heavenly video that will show me all the ways that God protected me in my lifetime.

There is a story, maybe urban legend, of a believer named Fredrick Nolan. He lived in Africa during a time of persecution, and was fleeing his enemies. He sought shelter in a cave, and, in his exhaustion, expected his enemies to find him soon. As he awaited death, he saw a spider begin to weave a web across the entrance of the cave. Within minutes, the entire opening of the cave was filled in with the spider's art work. When Nolan's pursuers arrived, they wondered if he was in the cave. This notion was put to rest as they saw the unbroken web of the spider, and believed it could not have been woven since his entrance into the cave. Nolan escaped. As he realized his salvation, he is said to have proclaimed: "Where God is, a spider's web is like a wall. Where God is not, a wall is like a spider's web."[3] God's protection is always at work for God's own. It is often just a matter of recognizing it.

9. Safety and Fear in the Lord — Verses 117a and 120a

Hold me up, that I may be safe. . . . **TEV**: *Hold me and I will be safe. . . . 120a: My flesh trembles for fear of you . . . .* **TEV**: *Because of you I am afraid.*

Reading these two verses on the same morning, I was struck by both at the same time. I couldn't resist the tension created by these two very different ideas. Is God a God of safety, or is God someone we should fear? To me, the answer is very clear: God is God. When we try to squeeze God into a box to match our own ideas, we must always fall short. God does bring comfort and safety, and I have experienced that often. There have also been times when I was afraid of God's presence, usually because of something I had done or omitted doing.

As I read "hold me and I will be safe," I thought of George. George was a recent widower when I met him. My spouse and I visited him often, and he became a good friend. George was never able to put himself in the Lord's arms and care. He was never able to allow the presence of the Lord to bring him comfort and peace. George left this life alone, and I found out about his death in a way I hope never again to experience. I hope that the Lord is now holding George in his arms.

The idea of being held by the Lord should give us a great deal of comfort, peace, and strength. It's a beautiful thought. I never picture the person of Christ. I usually just see light, but I can put myself in the comfort of that light. There is another aspect of the Lord holding me that I want to explore briefly: the idea of the Lord helping me to hold my parts.

Christ can help us hold our tongues, to keep us from speaking in anger, to keep us from gossip and criticism, to keep us from complaining and murmuring, to keep us from putting our feet in our mouths. The Lord can hold our hands to guide and help us. The Lord can form a chain with leaders to help them lead others. The Lord can hold our feet so we don't rush in as fools. The Lord can even help us dam the hurtful thoughts that often pour through our minds like a flood.

Mostly, however, I see myself in the Lord's arms, being

held safe and protected, as a child on a loving parent's lap, or as a lamb in the arms of the shepherd. I think God has a big lap. Oh, to have been one of the children that were brought to Jesus, blessed and affirmed by his firm but gentle hands.

The beginning of verse 120 seems contradictory to the above idyll: "Because of you I am afraid." The Psalmist is not talking about fear as in reverence, although we certainly need a healthy serving of this. Our author is talking about shaking-in-your-pants fear. In our culture, it is easy to forget that God is not all sweetness and light. There is still the element of wrath in God's nature, and that is certainly to be feared. Fear of God should motivate us to obey God. Actually, a better motivator would be love, but, lacking that, fear can serve the same purpose until God fills our hearts with God's love.

As the Psalmist said in this lengthy writing, those who obey have nothing to fear from God. God's judgments are indeed fearful, but Christ has taken away the sting for those who believe and obey. Thank you, Lord, that in Christ we do not have to fear the judgment and wrath of God. Thank you, Lord, that for those who will receive, the cross is the judgment seat. Thank you that we can be safe in you.

This idea of being afraid is expressed only in this verse. The Psalmist did make other references to fear which pertain to reverence. In verse 38, the Psalmist asked that the Lord confirm the promise, which is for those who fear God. Verse 63 tells us that the Psalmist was a companion of those who fear the Lord, and these are the ones who keep God's precepts. Those who fear the Lord shall rejoice when they see the Psalmist, because he hoped in the Lord's Word, in verse 74. And in verse 79, the Psalmist invited those who feared the

Lord to turn to him, so that they may know the Lord's decrees.

10. Fairness — Verse 138

You have appointed your decrees in righteousness and in all faithfulness. **TEV***: The rules that you have given are completely fair and right.*

How many times in our lives have we said "it's not fair"? This complaint begins on the playground and continues through our lives in countless interactions. As we mature, we may not say it as often as when we were little, but we sure probably think it.

I guess it is possible that now, in this age of parity and political correctness, these words are heard less often. Children are not held back in school. More and more, attempts are made at clothing uniformity. Games are designed so that there are neither winners nor losers. And, for good or bad, in some school systems, grades are eliminated.

It is not a bad thing that we want all children to feel that life is fair, that they are just as good as any other children. Is this really what's happening? When someone proclaims lack of fairness, it usually means someone thinks someone else has gotten an advantage over them. This concept will never disappear, as much as we try to create an atmosphere of parity.

I think Abraham Lincoln used the following little anecdote: Call a dog's tail a leg. How many legs does a dog have? The usual response will be "five." The correct answer is "four." Calling a tail a leg doesn't make it so. Disguising unfairness as parity doesn't make it so.

In the **TEV**, the Psalmist called the Lord's rules fair and right. The NKJV uses the adjectival form of the NRS's righteousness and faithfulness. I think these terms are probably more appropriate. We are promised mercy, grace, righteousness, and justice. I haven't found anything in traditionally-translated texts that talks about God or God's attributes being fair, at least not as we usually understand the term. Very often, we see God's work as not being fair, but that is the result of grace. Fairness is in the eye of the beholder, and God's choices will often not be ours.

Justice, the word most closely approaching fairness, means we get what we deserve. Fortunately, through Christ, we don't have to experience justice. Jesus Christ has accepted the just deserts of humanity, and if we believe in him, the debt we owe for our sin is paid. We get life with the Lord, far more wonderful than anything we might deserve, and way more than fair. If we follow God's rules, the concept of fairness skips right out the door. I don't want "fair," I want grace, mixed with mercy.

The Psalmist addressed concepts of fairness, rightness, and justice numerous times in this psalm. In relation to God's law, we see the idea in verses 7, 62, 75, 106, 137, 144, **160**, 164, and 172. Speaking of the person of God, the Psalmist discussed rightness in verses **40**, 123, 137, **138**, and 142. In verse **121**, the Psalmist spoke of his own righteousness. It is good to be reminded that, as followers of Christ, Christ's own righteousness is imputed to us, and we have none of our own. Since fairness and rightness are aspects of God's faithfulness, we might consider that concept at this time also. The Psalmist felt that God, in his faithfulness, had humbled him, in verse 70. The Psalmist acknowledged God's faithfulness for all generations in verse 90. Because of God's faithfulness, the Psalmist made a choice of faithfulness, in verse **30**, and, according to verse 158, looked at the faithless with disgust.

11. Nearness of the Lord — Verse 151

Yet you are near, O LORD . . . .; **TEV***: But you are near to me Lord. . . .*

Let's start at the end of this phrase: Lord. What does that word mean? Let's consider some possibilities: the creator and ruler of all things; the One who brings life and death, good and bad; the One who gave his Son for our redemption; the One who sends His Spirit as our comforter, teacher, advisor, and protector; the One to whom all glory, honor, and praises are due. This same Lord is also the One who demands holiness; the One who demands obedience and holds accountable the disobedient; the One who is exalted over all; the One who has steadfast love; the One who will one day send his son in victory; the One who gives eternal life; the One from whose hand all things come. God is the One who cannot be understood; the Perfect One who makes perfect; the One who promises never to leave or forsake.

This very same Lord is near to us, above us, around us, within us. The Lord hears each word and each sigh; knows every thought and dream; sees every motion, action, and deed, good or evil. God senses every motive and experiences each emotion. The Lord goes with me into every corner, and provides light for my darkness. The Lord knows me better than any other, including myself. God knows what lies ahead in my path and I can trust in that. The Lord unwillingly participates in my sin, then rebukes and forgives, by heeding my confessions.

Through God's Spirit, the Lord sits quietly with me; calms my disturbances; guides my pen and fingers; chides my idleness; rebukes my errant thoughts and speculations; and comforts me in sorrow. God helps in my ministry by helping me prepare messages; speaking through me; and comforting others through me. God touches my body with healing and touches others through my touch. Even the unspoken cries of my heart do not go unheard.

The Lord provides me with understanding; gives me the desire to do right, and the option not to; gives me choices and is present to guide me if I choose God's way. The "nearness of the Lord" has meanings that I can't even imagine. The nearness of the Lord is symbolic of God's love, faithfulness, mercy, provision, and everything else that God represents.

12. Truth — Verse 160

The sum of your word is truth; and every one of your righteous ordinances endures forever. **TEV**: *The heart of your law is truth, and all your righteous judgments are eternal.*

I like the **TEV** word "heart" rather than the NRS word "sum." Think of all the implications of "heart": core, foundation, lifeblood; reason for; main focus; basis; what it is all about; that which brings life.

We have already looked at the idea of God's Word or Law. It is God's commandment, that which governs God's people. It is what the Lord desires, the precepts the Lord has made known. It is God's concepts, commands, and judgments.

God's Law is the foundation for the rule of all nature and existence; it is perfect and all controlling, unchanging and faithful.

So, this Law of the Lord is truth. Where deceit and untruthfulness are present, God's Law is not. The truthfulness of God is a foundation for God's Law. God never changes, so God's Law never changes. We can put our complete trust in this truth. The truth is not capricious; it is based on God's understanding, not ours.

The eternality of God's truth means that it has no beginning or end. This truth controls all that God is and does. God's judgments have always been and will always be. There is only one truth, centered in Jesus Christ [John 14:6]. This eternal truth is the foundation of God's law. Humanity has created lies that so many want to accept as truth. God's truth encapsulates love, wrath, justice, mercy, forgiveness, omnipotence, comfort, peace, hope, judgment, righteousness, completeness, and life. For those who abide in it, and let it abide in them, there is fullness and abundance.

"Many men go their way in the search for truth. There are few who find it. Wandering in the wilderness of their human reason they will not go to the Word of God which appears from the distance to be but a barren outcropping. The Lord Jesus himself said: ' . . . I thank Thee, O Father, Lord of heaven and earth, because thou has hid these things from the wise and prudent, and has revealed them unto babes' [Matthew 11:25]."[4] God's truth is the only truth worthy of our time and effort, and we will be greatly rewarded in our search.

In verse **43**, the Psalmist asked that the truth never be taken out of his mouth, that he be enabled to speak the truth at all times. In verse 142, the Psalmist affirmed that God's law is always true.

13. Lost Sheep — Verse 176

I have gone astray like a lost sheep; seek out your servant. .
. . **TEV***: I wander about like a lost sheep; so come and look*
for me, your servant.

Recently, I have discovered a pastor's prayer by J. Timothy Allen called "God of Israel is My Shepherd."[5] This is a beautiful poem which speaks of the pastor both as a shepherd under the Good Shepherd, and also as a sheep. These two roles present a dichotomy which is often difficult for both pastor and congregation. Congregations want their Pastors to be impervious to difficulties, to live perfect lives, to "have it all together." I love thinking of myself as one of God's sheep, and I love the calling of a shepherd. It is often difficult, however, to reconcile the two.

Sometimes I feel like a lost sheep, and I love thinking that God will look for me in my lostness. A lost sheep is separated from its owner. It is not a wild sheep, which has no owner. It is separated from its owner by its own actions, intentional or otherwise. The owner did not abandon the sheep.

The lost sheep has wandered away from other sheep and the protection that comes within the fold and flock. It is subject to untold dangers: being cast down (falling), wild animals, rocks, and weather. The sheep needs the comfort, safety, and protection of the flock and the shepherd.

The loving shepherd will always want to restore wayward sheep to the flock. The shepherd always realizes that the sheep is lost and will go to great lengths to restore the sheep, even abandoning, in a sense, the sheep that remain in the fold. The shepherd will not punish the sheep for wandering off, but the sheep may have suffered injuries during its wandering that may affect it the rest of its life. Once returned, the other sheep in the fold will acknowledge the return of the wandering sheep.

As I examined this passage, I recognized some ways in which I have wandered off. The overwhelming picture I saw, however, was that my flock was short two particular sheep, and I wondered if I had done all I could to bring them back. After reading this passage and writing, I shared the previous thoughts with this couple. I did not get any response, but maybe the Lord will use that which I have been given to help them understand. I believe some of these writings, given to me in my time of devotion, will be used to help others.

The Psalmist addressed straying in several verses. In verse 10, he asked the Lord not to let him stray from the Lord's commandments. He talked about the Lord's rebuke of those who wander from the commandments, in verse **21.** According to verse 110, the Psalmist would not stray from the Lord's precepts, even though people were trying to trap him. In verse 29, the Psalmist asked the Lord to put false ways away from him.

IV
HUMANITY'S RECEPTION OF GOD'S GIFTS

1. Happiness — Verse 1
Happy are those whose way is blameless, who walk in the law of the LORD. **TEV**: *Happy are those whose lives are faultless, who live according to the law of the Lord.*

On the wall in a previous study, I had a poster-board list, where I had written things that, to me, indicate "What New Life in Christ Looks Like." Off the lower right-hand corner, I fastened two pictures: groups of deacons from two different bygone eras, with one similarity. In both pictures, the men look stern, even angry, and unhappy. Above these pictures I wrote "not like this."

In the church today, we talk too little about the joy and happiness that should come from being in relationship with Christ. Many people feel that the weight of following Christ is so demanding and ponderous that there is no room for joy. This is a sad corruption of what it means to follow Christ. These same people will give what can only be lip service to the idea of blessings that come from the Lord. Joy is one of the greatest blessings, yet it is as rare in the church today as bootstraps.

We've probably all heard of "sinless perfection," an imaginary concept purportedly attained by following a lot of legalistic don'ts such as don't dance, don't drink, don't play cards, and so on, ad nauseam. These man-made rules neither build us up nor glorify God. This legalism has chased many people away from the church, and gives the world unrealistic expectations of what Kingdom people should be.

Scripture talks about perfection, but it should be understood in the sense of being spiritually mature, and continually growing in the Lord. Jesus tells us to be perfect as our heavenly Father is perfect [Matthew 5:48]. There is little doubt that God is perfect. While we can find completeness and maturity in God, we will never, in this life, reach the perfection of doing everything absolutely correctly, especially not the following of man-made rules. When we turn to Jesus Christ, we are given the Holy Spirit. Through this Spirit, we have the power to choose God's way over our way and to carry out our choice. When we choose God's way, joy and happiness should be part of our life.

God's Spirit serves several functions in Kingdom life: (1) we are given power to believe through the Spirit's quickening; (2) we are convicted when we do wrong; and (3) we are given the power to do right. It is through God's Word that we know the right thing to do. Kingdom citizens become "faultless" not because of their own efforts, but because of Jesus Christ. When we put our faith in Jesus, our sin is forgiven. When we fall short of God's way, and confess this, our shortcoming is forgiven and we are cleansed [1 John 1:9].

It is my opinion that Kingdom people can live pure, faultless lives. Too often we choose not to. We want our way, and only when it is too late will we realize the blessings and joy we miss by not going God's way.

The first two verses of this Psalm communicate the "happiness" of following the Lord's ways, and these verses are the keystone for the whole passage. Another word for happiness, as we see in the beatitudes, is blessedness. When we follow the Lord's ways, our life will be blessed with many things, as this passage demonstrates. We will see that safety, life, joy, comfort, and righteousness are blessings of obedience.

This idea is expressed in verse 56, where the Psalmist talked about the blessing that has befallen him because of obedience. I experienced this very recently. As I was sitting with a family anticipating the approaching death of a loved one, I felt that I was to send my spouse home and stay with the family. I left with my spouse. The congregant died several hours after I left, and I did not find out about it until fourteen hours later. Had I stayed, I could have been a source of comfort to the family and known about the death significantly earlier. That same week, I felt that I was not to go to Albany with my spouse. At the last moment, I was tempted to go, but didn't. Had I gone with him, we both would have been stranded in Albany when his car broke down. Instead, the Lord blessed me not only by enabling me to be home with access to all the right numbers, but by having the repair work done that same day. Had I been disobedient, things would have been much more difficult. Obedience pays off.

Verse 162 tells us that the Psalmist rejoiced at the Lord's Word, even more than in great treasure. Obedience may not bring us wealth, but it can bring us joy that transcends earthly treasures. We see, in verse 174, that the Lord's law is delightful. I hope you have discovered this. We can't truly rejoice or find delight in disobedience. These are words of blessing and happiness, and they come from following God.

2. Purity — Verse 9

How can young people keep their way pure? By guarding it according to your word. **TEV***: How can a young [person] keep [their] way pure? By obeying your commands.*

Concepts such as chastity and abstinence of any kind seem to have gone the way of the dinosaur. We don't want to be told not to do something or that we can't have something. We live in an age that allows us to indulge our pleasures, regardless of where that indulgence leads. "Everybody is doing it (whatever "it" may be)," so why shouldn't we?

As a youngster, I sure didn't appreciate being stifled in my desires, especially when the reason given was that it "was for my own good." I wanted something and my parents didn't want me to have it, as far as I could tell. "Because I said so" were words often heard in my childhood. It took my own era of parenthood to understand that something I may have been prevented from doing or having may indeed have been for my own good.

As God's children, we may often feel the constraints placed upon us. When God gives us a directive, it is always for our own good. While we aren't subjected to lists of rules, clearly some things are wrong, and God's Spirit will convict us of making bad choices. As youth, barely beginning our Kingdom lives, we may not feel the Lord's correction as strongly as when we are more mature.

Following God's way will indeed help keep us pure. If we love the Lord with all our being, we will want to please the Lord. If we love others as ourselves, we will not harm. In this particular context, that means we will not degrade, humiliate, or abuse. We will understand the meaning of "no!" We will respect the wishes of others, but never to the extent that we allow ourselves to be led into sin.

When young people are feeling hormone-induced urges, and their dates want to resist, one response of the urger might be "don't take yourself so seriously." As children of God having the desire to obey God, we should take ourselves and our relationships very seriously. Those who refuse to take our desire for obedience seriously will be better left out of our lives.

No other verse in our psalm talks about purity, but it is significant here to mention our way of life. As seen in verse 1, it can be faultless. In verse 30, we see that the Psalmist chose the way of faithfulness. I discuss **choice** later.

Verses 101, 104, and 128 address the Psalmist's hatred of following the wrong way. We will look further at the concept of **hatred**, especially as it refers to people, which is not a Christian concept. The hatred of things, however, is a different story. There are many things in this life we should hate, because God hates them. Those who choose evil as a way of life are not living according to God's ways. We must hate and avoid evil ways if we are going to walk in the way of the Lord.

3. Arrogance and Pride — Verse 21

You rebuke the insolent, accursed ones, who wander from your commandments. **TEV**: *You reprimand the proud;*

cursed are those who disobey your commands.

God loves humility. When we can put aside our desire for control and submit to God, letting God be in control, we will reap the greatest blessings. We can't do this when pride or insolence takes charge. Pride deceives and is in itself a deceit. Pride says "look what I did" or "look what I have." Pride always points to self, not to others and especially not to the Lord, who is the source of all we do or have.

I like the story about the pompous farmer showing his handiwork to a young boy. He talked about all his earthly accomplishments before becoming a farmer, earning far more money than needed to purchase the farm. Then he pointed to the stacked hay, full granary, and boxes of produce and declared, "And I grew it all by myself, sonny. Started with nothing and now look at it." "From nothing?" echoed the duly impressed lad. "That's right," said the man, "From nothing." "Wow," the young boy said, pausing to reflect for a few seconds. "My dad farms, but he needs seed to grow his crop."[6]

The commandment to love is, by its very nature, a commandment to submit, both to the Lord and to others. If we can't submit to God, it is impossible to love God with all our being. If we can't submit to others, we can't think of their needs before our own and we certainly can't consider them better than ourselves. In pride, our service to others will be tainted with condescension, wrong motives, and incompleteness. This is not obeying the commandment to love.

When we have too much pride to love, we miss much blessing. This is the effect of cursedness. Too much pride, however, can also keep us from recognizing that we are sinners.

If we don't see ourselves as sinners, then it seems impossible to believe in and appreciate what Christ did on the cross. That will keep us from being saved, which will indeed curse us.

In verses 51, 69, 78, and 85, the Psalmist made clear his belief that the arrogant are people who are against the ways of God and against the people who follow God's ways. The scorn, lies, and hateful acts of the arrogant did not cause the Psalmist to turn away from following God's ways. Those who do not love the Lord may often try to belittle or even harm those who do. When we have submitted to God, these attempts will not harm our faith and certainly should not affect our desire to be obedient. Our response to derision and ridicule is our witness to what we truly believe about God.

The heart of pride, insolence, and arrogance is that the person bearing such attitudes may think they know even more than God. This makes it a little difficult to follow God's ways. Only when we give up attitudes of superiority can we truly follow God and reap the blessings of that action.

Pride, in itself, is not always bad. We are not worms. We are beings created in God's image, and as such should take a certain pride in who we are. We should have a sense of pride in the fact that God made a wonderful sacrifice to draw us to the Deity, through Christ. It should enrich us to know that God sends the Spirit to guide us in following the Lord's way. It is only when this pride gets out of hand, when we begin to look to ourselves and away from God, that it becomes sinful.

There is an idea floating around that a loving God would not reprimand or punish "good people," "religious people," or however else you might want to describe Christians. We will look at this idea a little later on. Our Psalmist certainly knew the *chastisement* of God, along with the blessings brought by our response to God's discipline.

4. Delight in God and God's Word — Verse 24
Your decrees are my delight, they are my counselors. **TEV***: Your instructions give me pleasure; they are my advisers.*

Like the Psalmist, I receive pleasure from Scripture, instructions, admonitions, warnings and all. There are mornings I can't wait to just sit in my special chair and read often-read texts to see what new things the Lord has for me that day. I believe God does speak to us through meditation on the Word.

How wonderful is the God who makes sure that those who follow and desire to serve are not left without guidance? It is all in the palm of our hands. Additionally, Jesus sent God's Spirit to enrich our understanding. How much more blessed are we than the Psalmist who, even under Law, could sing of God's great work and instruction?

Some form of delight is expressed throughout this Psalm. In verse 14, the Psalmist expressed more delight in following the Lord's commandments than in having great wealth. This idea is repeated in verse 162, where the Psalmist expressed as much joy in the Word as in finding great treasure (spoil).

Because of the pleasure the Psalmist professed in God's laws, in verse 16 we see a vow not to forget the commands. The Psalmist asked the Lord to help him be obedient to the commandments in verse 35, because of the happiness which he found in God's law. This thought continues in verse 47, where the author found pleasure in obedience because of his love for God's law.

Verse 70 refers back to the "arrogant" people of verse 69. The hearts of the arrogant are described as being fat and gross. There is an image throughout Scripture which indicates that fatness of heart is a deterrent to absorption of understanding. The lack of understanding of those who do not follow God would not deter the Psalmist's delight.

Recognizing his own imperfections, the Psalmist asked for mercy in verse 77. Our author expected life in exchange for his faithfulness to and joy in the Lord's instruction. This indication of expectation continues in verse 174, where we see a plea for saving help. The salvation needed at this time may be physical or spiritual, but the writer related this expectation to the delight he found in God's law.

While this is the only place where God's decrees are described as counselors, in verse 99 we see the assertion of the Psalmist that because of his meditation on the Lord's instruction, he had more understanding than all of his teachers. He had trusted in God's law to teach him, and, according to verse 108, saw God himself as the teacher. Because of this, he had gained greater knowledge and wisdom than that acquired from people who had not put as much trust in and received as much joy from God's law.

5. Choice — Verse 30

I have chosen the way of faithfulness; I set your ordinances before me. **TEV**: *I have chosen to be obedient; I have paid attention to your judgments.*

Obeying God is a very intentional act. We are not born with the ability to obey; we don't inherit the desire from our parents. Obedience, done out of a sense of duty and not love, is not true obedience, but it can be a start. The Psalmist may have put the cart before the horse here. It seems the path to obedience might begin by paying attention to God's judgments and indeed to all of Scripture.

As we immerse ourselves in Scripture, we see the faithfulness of God throughout. We see the benefit of following God's judgments. Authors introduce us to figures who demonstrate the results of both disobedience and obedience. As we study the admonitions of the epistles and put them to work in our lives, we should have even more evidence of God's faithfulness.

Faith is progressive: the more we believe and see the fruit of our belief, the more faith we receive. The same principle applies to obedience. When we see the fruit of the obedience of ourselves and others, we should be instilled with a desire to be even more obedient. It is a choice we make, and will be one of the most important choices of our life.

In verse 173, the Psalmist rightly expected God's help because of his choice. When we choose God's ways, we are not being arrogant to think that we might get special favor from God. We see this concept fulfilled throughout Scripture.

6. Eagerness — Verse 32

I run the way of your commandments, (for you enlarge my understanding.) **TEV**: *I will eagerly obey your commands, (because you will give me more understanding.)*

I want to play with the idea of eagerness as used in the **TEV**. This idea is interpreted in the idea of "running" in other translations. When we are eager, when we can't wait to get somewhere or see something or someone, we speed things up to make that encounter happen. To be eager means to act with quickness, to look forward to something. We look forward with joy, with a sense of anticipation. We give the effort the best we can.

The Psalmist demonstrated eagerness to obey God's commands. He wanted to do it to the best of his ability and without delay. He followed God's precepts without complaint, cheerfully and quickly. He wanted to fulfill what he knows God would have him do with all his heart and being. We see this same idea conveyed in verse **60**.

7. Desire — Verse 36

Turn my heart to your decrees, and not to selfish gain. **TEV***: Give me the desire to obey your laws rather than to get rich.*

This is the only passage in which the Psalmist asked for the desire to obey. Desire is mostly assumed throughout the passage. The Psalmist understood that God knew his heart, even when things might not have been going well.

The way I often put myself to sleep is by creating a fantasy in which I have great wealth. This wealth is always situated in such a way as to do lots of good for lots of people. In this daydream, I live quite well, but I am always challenging myself with the idea of sin.

God is not against wealth. 1 Timothy 6:10 says that it is the *love* of money that is the root of evil, not money itself. Kingdom work gets done through those who have and give money for the Lord's work. The motive for these gifts must be right:

a love for the Lord, not a love for being recognized for giving.

My husband and I have a relative who uses her wealth to help many people. Unfortunately, she gives away her money not for love of God or others. Her motive is not entirely clear, but she is indeed driven to charity. There have been—and I'm sure still are—people who have used great wealth for God's purposes. L.G. LeTourneau, the heavy equipment mogul, is one example who comes to mind.

Wealth can blind and impair. In the fantasy I create, I see myself as a nice person, but rarely active in church. Even in my imagination, my wealth, not God, is my focus. When one has great wealth, it would seem natural to begin to rely on that wealth rather than the One who provided it. When wealth becomes a stumbling block, impairing our relationship with the Lord, then it is better to be poor. To the Psalmist, faithfulness to God was preferred over wealth.

Poverty, however, is not a guarantee of following the Lord. In dire need, many will turn to any source that seems to provide some relief. The Psalmist knew great need and great wealth, and chose faithfulness to the Lord over all. God meets our needs, and if we walk in obedience and faithfulness, we will most likely see additional blessings in both the material and spiritual realm. When a conflict arises between wealth and obedience to God, the one who chooses God will always come out ahead, in this life and the next.

We also see references to wealth in verses 14, 72, and 127. In verse 14, the Psalmist took more delight in obedience than in great wealth. The assertion in verse 72 is that the law itself meant more to the Psalmist than all the money in the world. This idea is set forth in verse 127, where the Psalmist professed to love the Lord's commandments more than fine gold.

There is also in the Psalmist's plea for desire an anomaly rarely seen, but refreshing. As some read the Old Testament, it might be easy to perceive Israel as automatons, having no will of their own, marching to the beat of the Maker with no thought except to rebel. The Psalmist did not follow this pattern. The Psalmist asked for the desire to obey. Things go much easier when we really want to do them rather than when we are pushing against the grain.

The desire to obey is the first step to success. It is a step God can honor, and, as we begin to follow God, the desire to obey may be all we can produce. Don't be discouraged. God knows our hearts, and if the desire remains, God will send the Spirit to help fulfill the desire. Praise be to the Name of the Lord.

8. Paying Attention — Verse 37

Turn my eyes from looking at vanities; (give me life in your ways.) **TEV**: *Keep me from paying attention to what is worthless; (be good to me as you have promised.)*

The focus on this passage came at the pinnacle of the college basketball season. I love sports, and watch them on TV as often as possible, not being in a location to attend live events very often. Unless it is a really special game, however, I am usually busy doing something else as the game progresses. Many may see sports as a worthless activity. To me, sports are a celebration of the abilities God has given to others. It is a shame that these abilities are so often abused, or that the ability used to perform on the field is overshadowed by wrong choices and poor behavior off the field.

The Psalmist asked God for help in properly directing his attention. He recognized that God is in control. God can give more faithful desires. As we seek to further please the Lord, desires to do unpleasing things should diminish in our lives. God can help us in our determination to do only that which is edifying and pleasing.

To pay attention to something is to focus on it, to make it a priority over other things occurring at the time. When we focus on one thing, we tend to take our eyes off of other things. If we give all of our attention to sports or video games, or a romantic interest, or anything else, we are giving less attention to God. The Psalmist asked for help in focusing on those things which are most important to the Lord.

Whether or not something is worthless or vanity could be a subjective thing. I do not think sports are worthless, but know that others give them no thought. Some people think that attendance at church is a useless activity, but I believe that the Christian life can't properly be lived without it. I guess it all boils down to what God thinks, and we won't know that until we enter eternity.

The idea of paying attention, focusing, looking at or eyeing something is also dealt with in verses 6, 15, 18, 82, 123, and 148. In verse 6, the Psalmist asserted that paying attention to the Lord's commands would keep him from shame, the shame of defeat, of loss, of death. Meditation on the Lord's laws will help one fix his or her eyes on the Lord's ways, according to verse 15. The Psalmist, in verse 18, asked that his eyes be opened so that he could see all the wondrous things contained in the Lord's law.

The eyes of the Psalmist grew weary, according to verse 82, as he watched for the fulfillment of the Lord's promises and asked about help from the Lord. This idea of searching or waiting for the Lord to act is not anomalous in the psalm, but it is not the main theme. The beginning of this section (*kaph*) expressed the idea of neglect and abandonment by God, but in the end the Psalmist affirmed the Lord's constant love. Again, in verse 123, the Psalmist spoke of eyes tired from watching for the Lord's saving help. The *Qoph* section (verses 145–152) is another prayer for deliverance, but also ends in affirmation of God's presence and permanence. Within the *Qoph* section, verse 148 talks about the eyes of the Psalmist being open all night as he meditated on the instruction of the Lord.

Vanity or worthlessness is dealt with also in verse 118. The Psalmist believed that the plans of those who do not obey are in vain. This is what the author wanted to avoid by being obedient to God.

9. Speaking the Truth — Verse 43
Do not take the word of truth utterly out of my mouth. . . .
TEV: *Enable me to speak the truth at all times. . . .*

The Psalmist asked that he be enabled to speak truth. That was something I had to do as I grew in my walk with the Lord. My natural tendency was not to speak the truth, and I don't think anyone is born with a compulsion to always speak the truth, unless it is part of a psychological impairment.

We need help speaking the truth, and that help comes from the Lord. Philippians 4:13 tells us that we can do all things through Christ who strengthens us. If I trust the Lord to help me, I know that help will be forthcoming. God will enable us to do those things by which God is glorified. God's help will guide us in overcoming our natural tendencies.

Many people today want to know: what is the truth? How many truths are there? Jesus tells us that he is the way, the truth, and the life [John 14:6]. If we are looking for eternal truth, we need only look to Jesus.

When we talk about speaking the truth, we need to speak the truth of what we know. It is easy to embellish, to expand on the truth, but when we honestly desire to speak only that which we truly know, we set a goal for our lives that can't be matched. The truth is not what we think, perceive, hope, wish, imagine, or fantasize. It is what we know.

Sadly, some folks don't always want the truth. Truth is often painful, difficult to face, and we don't like pain. Often, even speaking in love, we have to speak things others may not want to hear. That does not lessen the requirement on us to speak it.

Jesus said that the truth will set us free. I long for the freedom that comes from knowing—and living—the truth of Christ. Do I have it all now? No. None of us will ever have all truth until we see the Lord. But I can live within the truth I know, and know the truth of Christ that brings freedom into my life now.

How does truth bring freedom? We can live within the truth that we can't please everyone, and thus stop trying to. We can recognize that we are not perfect, and stop trying to be. We can recognize that Christ can be a real part of our lives and thus know that we are never alone, and can enjoy all the benefits of knowing Christ. These are only a few of the ways in which we truly can be set free by knowing the truth.

When we know the truth, we must speak it and speak it in love. Nothing is more shameful than to hear someone speak the truth in order to hurt another. Love doesn't intentionally hurt another. Love sometimes has to speak unpleasant things, but not with the idea of showing another up or hurting another. Unpleasantries will be spoken only with the goal of building up, correcting, and encouraging. Even so, we know that the truth will not always be accepted.

Speaking the truth at all times means even when it is not convenient. When the truth hurts, embarrasses, causes relational difficulties, or puts others off, we are still obliged to speak it. There are times, however, when we can remain silent rather than speak a truth that brings difficulty, and we ought to work to take advantage of these opportunities. The secret lies in trusting the Lord. God's Spirit will guide us, if we seek guidance, in knowing when to speak and when we can be silent. Silence, however, is never appropriate if it gives the impression that we are agreeing with a lie.

The verse continues:

. . . for my hope is in your ordinances.

TEV: . . . Because my hope is in your judgments.

If I do not speak the truth at all times, I can't expect God's favorable judgment at any time. If I always speak the truth by God's enabling, no matter how unacceptable to some, I have the confidence that God will judge me righteously. It is about God and God is always to be glorified.

Speak, Mouth: In verse 13, we have the promise to declare the ordinances of the Lord's mouth. In verses 72 and 88, the Psalmist referred to the law as coming from the Lord's mouth.

In verse 46, the Psalmist talked about speaking of God's decrees before Kings. The Psalmist, in verse 103, described the Lord's Words as "sweet as honey in his mouth." The Psalmist pants with open mouth in longing for the Lord's commandments, according to verse 131.

Truth: In verse 142, the Psalmist declared the Lord's law to be truth; the Psalmist stated this a little differently in verse 160 by saying that the sum of the Lord's Word is truth. In verse 151, the Psalmist extolled the Lord's nearness and the truth of the Lord's commandments.

10. Freedom, Liberty — Verse 45

I shall walk at liberty, for I have sought your precepts. **TEV**: *I will live in perfect freedom because I try to obey your teachings.*

This verse is closely related to verse 43, being in the same section. When Jesus says that the truth would set people free, we have to remember that Jesus was speaking in Kingdom terms. It can't be denied that there are many people living in many varieties of physical captivity and oppression who know the truth of the gospel.

Let's consider what the Psalmist might be talking about as he addressed the freedom that comes from obedience. When we submit to someone's rule, we become subject to them. The identity of the ruler determines the extent of subjection. If we submit to a tyrant or a false god controlled by human forces, we may find that we have very little freedom. When we submit to a loving God who desires our best and knows that our obedience is the path to maximum benefit, we should see a different result.

God's law is a law of love. We are to love: God first, then others as our selves. Even before we love, however, God loved. Christ came to manifest God's love to all humanity.

Love is not centered in lots of rules. As we learn to love God, the love in our heart expands to others. If we continue seeking God, we will find that love has become a way of life. The love of God, flowing into and through us, transcends our earthly circumstances. We might be imprisoned or oppressed as an individual or a group, but if God's love is circulating within us, we cannot be held captive.

The freedom Jesus spoke of is not generally a freedom from physical forces, although it could be. It is greater than that. We should do what we can to free people from oppression, tyranny, and abuse. If we are not able to do that, we should not feel we have failed. If we have given people love, if we have shared the truth of a God who loves them and wants their love, we have helped them take a great step toward their freedom.

The freedom of the gospel can be seen in several incidents of the new church. Acts 5:41 tells us that the apostles, after being beaten, rejoiced in being able to suffer for the name of Christ. In Acts 16:25, we see Paul and Silas singing in prison, and the testimony of this freedom helped set the jailer free.

When we know the freedom of following a loving God, our hearts can't be bound. Our bodies may be beaten and tortured. Others may try to kill and destroy all that we hold dear. In spite of great oppression and abuse, many bear the testimony of hearts soaring in exaltation, because Christ has set them free, and they are free indeed.

The idea of freedom and liberty is not found in other verses in our Psalm. The idea of oppression—as the opposite of freedom—is discussed. In verse **121**, the Psalmist expressed the expectation of freedom from oppression because he had done what is right; he then asked for a guarantee of well-being from oppression in verse **122.** In verse 134, the Psalmist reversed the process, asking for freedom from oppression in order that he might keep the Lord's precepts.

11. Urgency — Verse 60

I hurry and do not delay to keep your commandments. **TEV**: *Without delay, I hurry to obey your commands (some similar thoughts on verse 32).*

I became a Christian in 1982, and I attended church prior to that. For about fifty years, I have heard about the impending return of Christ and the end of life as we know it. Like many others, I wait with great anticipation.

Recently on a science show, I heard that if earth's life were a twenty-four hour clock, the history of humanity would be the last two seconds. To accept this theory would mean to believe that the earth was formed from cosmic forces billions of years ago. Life itself came from the "scum" of the earth, the microbes that gathered and joined together in pools of water. Humanity is the far distant descendant of these gatherings. Personally, I don't accept this theory. I believe humanity was more intelligently planned, created and gifted, and not the result of mere chance.

Let's get back to the time question. In light of eternity, our time here is indeed a blink, or a sneeze, or a hiccup, however you choose to look at it. We are not the center of the universe and our time is barely noticeable on the eternal spectrum.

That is exactly why there is urgency in the need to obey God's commands. First, we need to make an eternal impact. When we spend our blink of time obeying God by loving God and loving others, we leave an eternal footprint. When we touch one person with love, that touch will very often travel through that one to others, and through them to even more people. There can be an enormous eternal impact from one act of obedience.

Secondly, I really do believe that Jesus will return some day, and we don't have a clue when that will be. We therefore need to be hurrying up and sharing God's love with as many people as we can while we can. We want the world to be ready for the return of its Savior, so we need to be always busy.

There is a third reason for urgency in obeying God's command: God is worth it. When my husband or anyone else wants me to immediately jump to comply with their request, I tend to balk. Not so with God.

God deserves our immediate response to those things which are impressed upon our hearts. We must learn to act on God's time, not our own. When laziness, stubbornness, or any other negative response appears, we block the blessing of immediate obedience. Who knows what that blessing might have been?

In verses 19 and 54, the Psalmist addressed his brief time on this earth. Because of his belief, he asked God not to hide his commandments from him, and declared that he spent his brief time composing songs about the Lord's commands.

12. Wisdom and Knowledge — Verse 66

Teach me good judgment and knowledge, for I believe in your commandments. **TEV**: *Give me wisdom and knowledge, because I trust in your commands.*

Are followers of Christ wiser, smarter, and more knowledgeable than non-believers? Non-believers might have tons of book learning, but a follower might have that also. Non-followers can also be wise. It might be helpful to look at the two aspects of understanding: wisdom and knowledge.

Wisdom: I believe this comes from God, not books. It includes discernment, which is a gift of God's Spirit. It might be seen as in innate knowing, but I don't think we are born with it. We might be born with common sense, a more "common" term for wisdom. I feel I was born with discernment. I distinguish this natural talent from a spiritual gift of discernment of spirits.

When we follow God, however, I believe that through the work of the Holy Spirit, God enhances what we might have naturally, and gives us supernatural gifts. These are rightly called the gifts of the Spirit, and include such things as giving, healing, tongues, and gifts of power. These are all given for the benefit of the Church, not for individuals.

Christians—true believers—should not be scatter brains. God gives order and focus, and is not a God of chaos. Those naturally scatterbrained should receive focus and observe a change in their thinking abilities as they grow in the Lord. This is one example of God changing a natural endowment. Followers of Christ should indeed show a greater amount of wisdom and discernment. They should be people sought out by others. They should be cautious in giving advice, but Spirit-filled advice can usually be followed.

A danger might be crediting oneself with wisdom rather than the Lord. What may start out being the Holy Spirit might become too much of us, resulting in great danger and damage. We must always trust in God's commands, and give God the glory.

Knowledge: This is what we learn from being taught, whether by books, directly from others, or from experience, although experiential learning may border on wisdom.

When I first came to the Lord, God told me that I was to "learn from no man." Rather than understanding the sexist implications, I took that word to my heart to mean that God was to be my teacher. As I read Scripture, the Holy Spirit would teach me. Indeed, as I participated in Sunday School and other discussions, it seemed apparent to others and me that I was learning very quickly.

Since the early years of my Kingdom walk, I have lived by this instruction, so I questioned my very clear call to seminary. Wouldn't I be learning from people? In retrospect, I know that what I learned came from my own work, my own searching of texts, and the formation of thoughts for papers based on what I learned. God continued to be the teacher.

I am not a super-knowledgeable person. I think the Lord would give me knowledge if I would read more. But I want, first of all, to know Scripture as a basis for my life and work. I trust the Lord to lead me to other sources for my edification and ministry.

I do believe followers of Christ have more wisdom and the potential for more knowledge than non-followers. We just too often fail to access all that is available to us. Recently I preached a message on Spiritual gifts. As I lingered on wisdom and knowledge, I realized that there were some in the sanctuary who had these gifts, but for various reasons had suppressed their use. We need to use what God has given us to God's honor and glory and for the edification of the church.

The Psalmist asked for understanding of the Lord's precepts, in verse 27, in order that he might meditate on them. In verse **32**, the Psalmist would obey because God had given understanding. Understanding will lead to better obedience, according to verse 34. Because the Lord created the Psalmist, he could expect understanding to help him learn, in verse 73. Because of the understanding the Psalmist was given, he hated wrong, according to verse 104. As a servant of the Lord, the writer asked for understanding to know the teachings of the Lord, in verse 125. In verse 130, we see the concept of light coming from understanding. In verse 144, we see that because the Lord's concepts are just, the writer could expect life through understanding. The Psalmist cried for help and understanding, according to verse 169, and trusted the Lord's promise.

13. Joy in Suffering — Verse 92
If your law had not been my delight, I would have perished in my misery. **TEV**: *If your law had not been the source of my joy, I would have died from my sufferings.*

I was not raised in a church. In my pre-teen years, my parents sent my brother and me to a nearby church, but it was not a family affair. I did just about everything a youngster my age could do in a church, but what I may have brought home from church was not, in my mind, reinforced at home.

As time went on, I began identifying what, in my spiritually-unformed mind, seemed to be hypocrisy. In my mid-teen years, I dropped out of church. What hypocrisy did I witness? The example that sticks in my mind is of youth leaders who barely cleared the doors of the church before lighting a cigarette. I grew up in a home filled with cigarette smoke, but it just seemed wrong at church.

I was a wild, rebellious teenager, and began getting into trouble. As a single parent, in my early twenties, I began an on-again, off-again relationship with church. I could take it or leave it. For years I continued in this pretend state. I call it pretend because people thought I had a relationship with the Lord. I didn't and I knew I didn't. I was always aware that something was missing.

In 1982, at the age of 34, that indifference stopped. I entered into a relationship with Christ, and my heart changed. The feeling that something was missing disappeared. At the same time, some things in my life changed, and I entered what I still refer to as my most difficult years. Through the difficulty, however, a marvelous thing happened: I learned more about the Lord and the joy, peace, and comfort that could come even through dire circumstances.

First, I lost a job that paid well. Then my teenage daughter, whom I had been single-parenting, began demonstrating to me what I had put my own parents through. Financial and relational problems piled one on the other. My salvation was my relationship and time with the Lord.

During the work week, I took little devotional time. I attended Tuesday visitation and Wednesday dinner and Bible studies at the church I had joined. Of course on Sundays, I attended whatever the church had to offer. Saturday, however, was my power day. I would start my day reading Scripture and praying. There were times when hours passed apart from my awareness. Saturday—even above Sunday—was the day I looked forward to, the day in which I took great joy in my time with my Lord and what I brought away from that time. Because of this period, I continue to be a strong advocate of personal devotional time, no matter one's calling in life. For a pastor especially, it is essential.

I know now that those dark times were preparatory and essential for my spiritual growth. Without the darkness, perhaps I would not have been so driven to spend that time in the Light. In any case, I not only learned vast amounts of Scripture, but I avoided spiritual death. God used difficulty and defeat to draw me closer and to strengthen and prepare me for what lay ahead for me.

The Psalmist expressed the idea of joy in many ways within this Psalm. In verse 14, he declared his delight above all riches. He delighted in the Lord's statutes and would not forget them, according to verse 16. As we saw in verse **24**, his delight in God's instruction elevated those instructions to the level of being his advisers. Because he found happiness in God's law, he asked for help to be obedient, according to verse 35. He obeyed because of his love for God's commands in verse 47. Although some had no understanding, he found pleasure in the law of the Lord, in verse 70. According to verse 77, he expected mercy and life because of his pleasure in the Lord's law. We see in verse **111** that the Lord's decrees were the joy of the Psalmist's heart. Verse **143** is on point with this focal verse, declaring that, despite trouble and anxiety, the Psalmist found joy in the commandments. The Psalmist's longing for the saving help of the Lord, because of his happiness in the law, is expressed in verse 174.

14. Trust — Verse 114

(. . .); I hope in your word. **TEV***: (. . .) I put my hope in your promise.*

So many things in this life are unreliable. Appliances, electronics, automobiles, stick-on lights, and, sadly, people, just can't always be depended on. That is why the promises of God are true treasures—if we are in right relationship and position to receive, we can always trust and hope in God's promises. From the promise of God's presence ever with us in this life—and all that promise entails—to the promise of eternal life through Christ, God's promises can always be received with hope and confidence. The promises of God are the *foundation and the reason* for a life of obedience, the *means* of living in obedience, and the *reward* for living in obedience.

It is difficult to distinguish between hope, trust, and faith. Hebrews 11:1 tells us that faith is the assurance of things hoped for, the conviction of things not seen. We can't see, touch, or hear God. By faith, however, we know that God is there and that we can believe and trust. We know this because of the examples in scripture of those who believed in God, and we know this because of our own experience. In a seminary class, I heard a professor say that you can't base a theology on experience. That may be so, but I can base faith on experience, and the reality of my faith is the only theology I need for daily living.

The Psalmist knew a lot about faith, hope, and trust. In verse 42, the Psalmist was able to answer those who taunted him because of his trust in the Lord's Word. His hope was in the Lord's ordinances, according to verse **43**, and he asked the Lord not to take the Word of truth from him. In verse 49, we see the Psalmist's request that the Lord remember the Word given, the Word in which the Lord had made him hope. In verse **81**, even though his soul languished for God's salvation, his hope continued. The Psalmist knew that the promises of the Lord bring life, and he asked not to be put to shame because of his hope in those promises in verse 116. As he cried for help before dawn, the Psalmist still put his hope in God's Word in verse 147. In verse 166, the Psalmist proclaimed his hope in the Lord's salvation as he fulfilled the Lord's commandments. Through great difficulties, perhaps more than we will ever face, the Psalmist continued to trust and hope in all which God had promised and all which God had been to him.

15. Servanthood — Verse 125
I am your servant; give me understanding, so that I may know your decrees. **TEV**: *I am your servant. Give me understanding, so that I may know your teachings.*

This was the first verse I wrote on from this Psalm. At the time, I explored the concepts of "knowing" and "teachings" and I will share some of this next. The idea of servanthood is very important in Kingdom life, so I want to focus on this for a bit.

In a society that promotes and glorifies superiority and independence, servanthood is not a popular idea. It is related to equally unpopular ideas such as submission and relinquishment. We want to be our own bosses, the focus of our own lives. Turning our lives over to the control of another, especially another we can't see, hear, or touch, is not a comforting idea. Let's get over this! We can't properly live out Kingdom life unless we are indeed servants.

We easily say things like "Jesus is Lord." Do we really know what that means? In ancient times, lords controlled everything of those they lorded over. Subjects had no life of their own, no rights, few, if any, possessions. They lived, worked, and reproduced for others. That doesn't sound very appealing, does it?

I have always been headstrong and stubborn. I wanted my own way. Letting others have their way in my life was a huge hurdle to overcome. I am currently situated somewhere between the apex of the hurdle and the downside, still struggling to retain some control.

Allowing Christ to be lord of our lives makes perfect sense, if we could only grasp the implications. The Lord can deal with any situation, knows what lies ahead, and is prepared to walk with us through it. Nothing takes God, who knows us better than we know ourselves, by surprise. While we see snippets of life, the Lord sees the whole picture and how we fit into it. To submit to Christ's rule may cause some discomfort at times, but in the long run, what better thing can we do with our lives? Personally, without Christ, I did a pretty good job of messing up my life. I will continue to try to turn it over to Christ, who can only make improvements.

Christ, however, is not the only person we are called to serve. When we become Kingdom servants, we are to serve all others. That's where the rub comes, isn't it? We rationalize: well, some of these people may not know as much as we do, they may not be serving Christ as we are. They may not be very nice people. Maybe they don't even like us. Irrelevant, all irrelevant. We are called to serve all, and only when we do that can we consider ourselves servants. At a conference a while back, I invested in a wood carving of Jesus washing the feet of a disciple. It stays on my desk as a constant reminder to be a servant to others.

The Psalmist referred to himself as the Lord's servant in the following verses: 17, 23, 38, 49, 65, 76, 84, **122**, 124, 135, **140**, and **176**. One verse stands out on the subject of servant-hood. Verse 91 says that all things are the Lord's servants. All things. That means not only all people, but all nature, all inventions, all contrivances, even all thoughts are the servants of God. That boggles the mind. Sun and moon, storms, rivers, winds, trees and grass, lions, tigers, and bears, and robots are the Lord's servants. This should say a lot to us about God's control over the universe. He is indeed Lord, and yet Jesus himself took on the form of a servant as he came to visit humanity [Philippians 2:5–8].

Knowing: What does it really mean to know? Some individually-brainstormed thoughts: to be acquainted with; to be intimate with; to have a thorough understanding of; to put into practice—learning experientially; to be able to recite; to be able to teach; to be in relationship with; to be hidden in one's heart—heart knowledge vs. head knowledge; to treasure. When the Psalmist said that he wanted to know the Lord's teachings, he was saying, as we should say, that he wanted them to be a vital part of his life. The teachings should come to mind and speech as easily as breath. What a goal to set for our spiritual growth.

16. Love — Verse 140
Your promise is well tried, and your servant loves it. **TEV***: How certain your promise is. How I love it.*

When I was in junior and senior high school, I rode a school bus from the suburbs where I lived to school downtown. The blessing of this is that after school I could walk down to the theater my father managed. I loved those days. The promise of spending some time with dad was invigorating and antici-pated with great joy.

I always had the promise of afternoons and evenings with dad, and there was nothing I liked better. There has been no one in this life I loved more than my father. Times with him were very special. I too often was arguing with mom, but times with dad were precious and ended all too early.

It is easy to think of dad when I read this passage. The promise of time with dad was the joy of my life. I could al-ways count on him being there for me. Sadly, in years too soon coming, I would not be there for him. I let him down at a time when I could have been his biggest source of comfort.

If an earthly parent can make a promise of presence and keep it, as much as they are able, how much more precious are the promises of God? Dad left this life when I was 19. I have God's promise never to leave me nor forsake me. Dad never took parenting classes, but even if he had, there were times I would stray from his direction. I have no desire to stray from God's care and promise. Dad wasn't perfect and I adored him. God's promise and fulfillment are perfect, and more to be loved.

God's promises are as sure as the dawn and the setting of the sun. Too many times I have learned that obedience brings blessing and disobedience brings loss. I have no desire to disobey one who has so clearly promised me provision, protection, peace, and life. I want the promise of God's best in my life. I have seen the result and can love nothing less.

Besides obedience, what might our love of God entail? The first word that comes to mind is "belief." Throughout scripture we have examples of those who believed and we see the results. We also have the opposite. If God acted in one life centuries ago, I can believe God will similarly act in my life. I can believe that the admonitions set forth by Christ and in the Epistles are for me as much as for the people they were given to. Caveat here: scripture contains eternal truth and cultural situations. We must learn the difference before we claim every admonition of scripture.

The next word that comes to mind is "being." Being the presence of Christ; being an example of Kingdom life; being the best I can be are all aspects of my love for God. Doing is important, but many people put the focus on doing before being. I think being is the primary thing. If we are truly being all we should be in Christ, we will definitely be doing. The reverse does not hold true. Some folks get so busy doing that they have no time or energy to spend on being.

When we fall in love with someone, we want to find out everything about them that we can. We want to be with that person all the time. We think about them all the time. When I claim to love someone in this life—such as my spouse—I spend time with that person. I do things for that person, I talk to that person, and I talk to others about that person. These are all part of relationship. Relationship should also be an element of our love for God. We should have the same aspects of relationship with the Lord that we have with others we claim to love.

The Psalmist talked about love both from the point of view of God's love and human love. We will look at the passages dealing with God's love first. In verse 41, the Psalmist described the steadfastness of God's love, and pleaded for it. The Psalmist claimed that the earth is full of God's steadfast love in verse **64.** In verse 76, he claimed the promise of God for God's steadfast love to become his comfort. The author counted on the Lord's steadfast love to save his life in verses 88 and 159. The Psalmist counted on God's steadfast love in God's dealings with himself in verse 124. Because of God's steadfast love, in verse 149, the Psalmist expected the Lord to hear his voice.

It is significant to consider the word "steadfast" which accompanies every reference to God's love in our translation. In the Hebrew, this is the word *khesed*. The word is commonly used to describe the many aspects of God's love. It contains the ideas of mercy, kindness, loyalty, loving kindness, and unfailing love, and probably a few ideas we don't understand. The Psalmist knew all of these aspects, when he was obedient and when he was not. We can know this same unchanging love of God.

The Psalmist also talked a lot about his own love for God

and God's laws. As related in verse 47, the Psalmist delighted in the Lord's commandments because he loved them. This love led to reverence for the commandments in verse 48. Because of the Psalmist's love for the law, as described in verse 97, it became his meditation all day long. Verse 119 is anomalous to the Christian life, because of the statement by the Psalmist that he loved the Lord's decrees because the Lord counts the wicked of the earth as dross. This idea is hardly in keeping with the idea of valuing all others. Expressing a more appropriate sentiment in verse 127, the Psalmist declared his love for God's commandments to be greater than his love of fine gold. In verse 132, the Psalmist expected God to treat him with graciousness, as demonstrated toward all those who love the name of the Lord. The concept expressed in verse 165, that those who love God's law find great peace, is fulfilled to us through Christ. In verse 167, the Psalmist declared that his very soul kept God's decrees, because of his exceeding love for them.

It seems appropriate to address the subject of hatred within this section on love. Verses 104 and 128 are not very far from Christian thought: the understanding and direction the Psalmist got from God's precepts caused him to hate every false way, as we should also. Similarly, in verse 163, the Psalmist hated falsehood, but loved God's law.

Hatred of enemies, others, and self is not a Christian concept, but the Psalmist was writing under a different understanding of God's love than that demonstrated through Christ. The Psalmist's hatred was extended to people, according to verse 113, where the author averred hatred of the double minded. In verse 141, the Psalmist saw himself as small and despised, but still he did not forget God's precepts.

17. Joy and Delight — Verse 143

Trouble and anguish have come upon me, but your commandments are my delight. **TEV**: *I am filled with trouble and anxiety, but your commandments bring me joy.*

Nothing kills joy like taking our eyes off of Jesus and focusing on our circumstances and the events around us. We fret and fear; we feel lost and hopeless because we have become our focus. This just doesn't have to happen.

The greatest commandment is to love God. Start praising God to lift the spirit of heaviness that circumstances may have poured out upon you [Isaiah 61:3]. Start thinking about God and the ways you have seen God work. Sit quietly in God's presence (yes, God is indeed present). Read Scriptures that talk about God—the Psalms are a good place to start. Make sure you are living, speaking, and thinking in a way that pleases God. Doing these things should get you started on the upswing.

The second commandment is to love our neighbors as ourselves. Who can you help right now? Who has previously been touched by God through you? Remembering how we have seen God work is a great picker-upper. Is there someone you are at odds with? Go and do what you can to make it right. Are you angry about something? Chances are, another person is involved. Ask the Lord to help you bring peace in the situation. Consider other people more than yourself. Put others first!

Do you feel more joyful, more at peace? If you will do

just the things listed earlier, you should know joy and peace in increasing amounts. If there is no change, you might need to do a little soul archaeology. Dig down deep, to the very bedrock of your life, because most likely the fault is in your foundation. Have you truly believed God and are you trusting in his Son Jesus Christ? That is the basis for all the promises we have. Without the foundation—faith in Christ—we have no material with which to build. Make sure your relationship with God is right, then build on it by following the two commandments which envelop all others [Matthew 22:36–40]. You should begin to know not only joy and peace, but everything else God has to offer.

Even though he knew hardship, the Psalmist also knew the delight and joy of the Lord and the law of the Lord. In verse 14, delight in the Lord's ways was seen as being as great as in riches. The Psalmist promised never to forget a word of the statutes, in verse 16, in which he delighted. To the Psalmist, the Lord's decrees were a delight, even to the extent of being his counselors, in verse **24**. Because of his delight, the Psalmist asked to be led in the path of the Lord's commandments in verse 35. The delight came, according to verse 47, because of the Psalmist's love for the commandments. Even though the arrogant have fat hearts—the implication being their inability to follow the law—the Psalmist delighted in the law, in verse 70. In verse **111**, the Psalmist stated that the Lord's decrees were the joy of his heart.

There is an expectation, expressed in verse 77, that mercy and life will come to the Psalmist because of his delight in the law. Related to this is verse **92**, in which the Psalmist vowed that if he did not delight in the Lord's law, he would have perished in his misery. In verse 174, the Psalmist expressed longing for the salvation of the Lord, because the law was his delight.

18. Cry to the Lord — Verse 145

With my whole heart I cry; answer me, O LORD. I will keep your statutes. **TEV**: *With all my heart I call to you; answer me Lord and I will obey your statutes.*

The theme of the Psalmist's cry for help is repeated in the next two verses. It was a time of distress for the poet, and he knew that his help was only in the Lord. The promise of obedience is repeated in so many verses—and is, indeed, the theme of this whole Psalm—that we will only list the verses in which this promise is found, without description.

The call of the Psalmist was not a whispered plea, not a murmur. To me, calling speaks of a shout: I want your attention; I expect you to hear me; I believe you do. The Psalmist also expected a response. Why would he call to someone from whom he expected no response?

The cry of the Psalmist is not done passively. It is no watered down prayer for help. The entire being of the caller, all that he was, was put into this call. The call came in the Psalmist's sincerest manner and everything was directed toward the call. There is an element of the utmost urgency. God knows the Psalmist's heart, and therefore God knows the worthiness of the Psalmist to call upon him. The Psalmist did not let anything distract him in his call, and was not ashamed of calling on the Lord, who was the source of his help.

The call of the Psalmist was direct. He needed no intermediary. He could go directly to God. His cry was specific, he was not just whistling in the wind. He went directly to the source of the one who could help him with whatever his need.

It is only in this set of verses—specifically, verse 146—where the Psalmist called to the Lord. Often, to "call to" might just mean that one is voicing their emotions, without really seeking a response. We may feel angry, frustrated, hurt, or sad, and we just want the Lord to know it. This does not always eliminate the desire for a response, as we see in this passage, but more often it conveys feelings rather than need.

In most Scripture passages, when the caller wanted help from the called one, the phrase used is "call upon" rather than "call to." As this phrase is generally used, it meant that the caller definitely wanted the participation of the Lord in something. When we read the phrase "call upon," we can almost always read "help me," "save me," "protect," and "feed" me.

The Psalmist used the phrase "whole heart" in two ways: In verse 10, as in the present verse, he was seeking the Lord with his whole heart. In verses 34 and 69, he promised to follow the Lord with his whole heart. The Psalmist did not do anything half way. All that he had was put into seeking the Lord and obeying the Lord. May we be given the heart of the Psalmist.

We see the Psalmist calling to the Lord in the two verses following this passage and in verse 169, where the Psalmist voiced the plea that his cry come before the Lord, a more passive understanding. Interestingly enough, we don't see the Psalmist's request—or demand—to be answered in any other verses.

Promises to obey, keep, heed, follow, or observe are repeated in verses 8, 17, 32, 33, 34, 36, 44, 45, 80, 88, 106, 115, 129, 134, 146, 167, and 168. As stated before, this is the whole theme of this Psalm. The Psalmist knew the goodness of the Lord and his law, and the blessings of obedience, and he was committed to that.

19. Treasure — Verse 162

I rejoice at your word like one who finds great spoil. **TEV***: How happy I am because of your promises—as happy as someone who finds rich treasure.*

What does it mean to be happy? It means that we are joyful, content, elated, filled with pleasure, satisfied, blessed, not complaining, thankful, and praising. I recently heard a congregant say that she—and others—are not happy unless they are complaining. The truth is that if we are complaining, we are not happy. Happiness is a state of mind, usually based on our circumstances, and we can choose or reject it.

Rich treasure may be subjective: one man's garbage is another man's treasure. Generally, treasure means material wealth; it enriches life; it is the ability to help others. It means dreams fulfilled, resources, provision, value, and comfort. We desire treasure to change our lives, take us where we want to go, help us afford any service and convenience. Abundance can sometimes be misused, but when properly used it can touch and change many lives.

We have looked at the idea of God's promises previously. Some that we have in Scripture are salvation; hope of eternal life; presence; abundant life; peace; help; right place; victory; joy; freedom from fear; a prepared place; an advocate; a counselor; reward; comfort; inheritance; rest; strength; ability to fly (as in Isaiah 40:31); forgiveness; protection; provision; faithfulness; freedom from sin; new life; desires of the heart; and love. The Psalmist said that God's promises were treasures. They provide all we need and beyond. God's promises give us extraordinary capabilities, extended even into the supernatural realm.

God's promises fulfill the desires of the faithful heart, and come through faith in Jesus Christ. They are available to those who trust and obey. The promises of the Lord leave nothing lacking, although God's promises may be often misunderstood. God's promises are based on God's attributes: love, wrath, justice, mercy, faithfulness, etc. God's promises, like God, God's truth, and God's law are eternal.

We need never doubt God's promises. We claim God's promises when we are in right relationship. We may not always see God's promises as good, but if we love God, they will work or weave together for good. We often try to claim God's promises when we are not in right relationship or position, and we don't see their manifestation in our lives. This results in frustration, bitterness, doubt, rebellion, and separation.

God's promises are gifts, but they are not to be taken for granted. Christ died so that God's promises can be fulfilled in our lives. If we believe and are faithful in our lives, we will see the fulfillment of God's promises in our lives.

We see a comparison with wealth or riches in verse 11, a well-known verse which says the Psalmist treasured the Lord's Word in his heart. In verse 14, we are told that the Psalmist delighted in the way of the Lord's decrees as much as in all riches. This idea is continued in verse 72, where the law of God's mouth is better than "thousands of gold and silver pieces." Finally, in verse 127, the Psalmist declared his love for the Lord's commandments to be more than gold, more than fine gold.

20. Memory — Verse 176
. . . for I do not forget your commandments. **TEV***: . . . I have not neglected your laws.*

No matter what he faced, the Psalmist did not forget the Lord's laws. They were the foundation of his life. He lived to obey, and even when he strayed, he remembered that from which he had strayed. Sin can cause extensive memory loss. This did not happen to the Psalmist. Through all his troubles and woes, he remembered.

The idea of memory is addressed in many verses by the Psalmist. In verse 16, the Psalmist asserted his delight in the statutes and promises not to forget the Word. In verse 55, the Psalmist claimed to remember the Lord's name in the night. In verse 93, the Psalmist couldn't forget the Lord's precepts, because they brought him life. Because the Lord taught him, he could not turn away from the ordinances, in verse 102.

Through oppression by the wicked, the Psalmist did not forget the Lord's law, in verse 61. Although he had become like a wineskin in the smoke, according to verse 83, the Psalmist did not forget God's statutes. I am not sure of the imagery of the smoked wineskin. Although he held his life continually in his hand, in verse 109, the Psalmist did not forget the Lord's law. In verse 141, even though he felt small and despised, he did not forget the Lord's precepts. Finally, in verse 153, because he had not forgotten the Lord's laws, the Psalmist expected the Lord to rescue him from his misery.

V
HUMANITY ALONE

1. Weariness — Verse 81
My soul languishes for your salvation; I hope in your word.
TEV*: I am worn out Lord, waiting for you to save me; I place my trust in your word.*

Sometimes I feel so weary in dealing with some of the idiosyncrasies of the people I minister to. I have made several inquiries into other possible ministry positions. While doing so, I am seeking God's best in God's time. That means if God wants me to stay here and learn how to deal with the problems that make me want to leave here, I will trust the Lord to help me do that with the added ability to minister to these people.

Sometimes I really do feel worn out, even though my work load is rarely strenuous. The weariness I experience is not always because of the people I minister to. We take weird trips. We will drive hundreds of miles in a weekend to attend this meeting or that. The tiredness that comes from such activity adds to some of the frustration I experience in ministry. More and more I am realizing that I need some real vacation time. My idea of vacation or retreat is to go somewhere and relax. My spouse's idea of vacation is to be constantly on the move, with a different motel or camping spot each day, unless we are attending a meeting. Then full attendance at every activity is required.

I am often weary and tired, but it really isn't appropriate to say I am worn out. I know how to say "no"; I am quite comfortable, thank you, doing nothing. I take brief respites as I need them and trust the Lord to turn them into energy and productivity.

The Psalmist, from what we know about David, would have known the real meaning of being worn out. Running from Saul, then his own son Absalom; trying to manage a dysfunctional family; ruling a quarrelsome people would all cause anyone to seek salvation from the Lord. From other scriptural passages of course, we know that David finds comfort, wisdom, joy, and life in obeying the Lord and trusting God's Word.

Salvation from the Lord comes in many forms: eternal salvation comes through Christ on the cross. I believe God provides physical salvation, protecting us from other forces that would do us harm. When we trust God, we can count on being free from fear, worry, and discontent. God will certainly save us from our enemies, but I believe God also has to save us from ourselves. When we take on more than we can bear, when we don't take good care of our bodies, inside and out, when we take our eyes off the Lord and look at circumstances which have the potential to overwhelm us, then, like the Psalmist, we will indeed feel the pressures of life and cry out to the Lord to save us.

2. Limits — Verse 96

I have seen a limit to all perfection, but your commandment is exceedingly broad. **TEV**: *I have learned that everything has limits; but your commandment is perfect.*

This passage, with the semicolon after "limits" in the **TEV**, seems to indicate a separation between the two ideas. The "but" brings them back together. I prefer the **TEV** understanding with this verse. The commandment of the Lord is the only thing in this life that is perfect, but the NRS version seems to indicate that other things might reach a limited version of perfection.

Everything has limits. Can you think of anything that you perceive as not having limits? As I considered this verse, I listed a number of things that would be considered limited: (my) ability; understanding; physical life; financial resources; time with spouse and family; freedom; tolerance; acceptance; service; and love. With God, the limits can be extended indefinitely, but the possibility of reaching the limit always exists. We often reach our limit quickly, and we do not explore all potential limits, both because we are not trusting God.

We can do all things through Christ who strengthens us [Philippians 4:13]. Sometimes, however, we may be limited in how much of "all things" we can really do. How much will we trust the Lord? Does the Lord want us to do everything?

When it comes to love, God demolishes the limits. God's love to us is inexhaustible, and we can never love too much. Some things, like spoiling children, we do too much of, and call love, but that is not really love.

Although there is a limit to the authority of all earthly kings, there is no limit to God's authority. Actually, nothing about God—steadfast love, justice, faithfulness, peace, strength, hope, comfort, etc.—(1) has limits; (2) is limited toward creation; or (3) can be understood to the limit. The exception to this lack of limits is God's tolerance for sin and unfaithfulness.

We can limit God's attributes toward us by sin, unbelief, and ignorance. It might be more accurate to say we limit the acquisition or assimilation of God's attributes by those attitudes. It is like damming up a free-flowing stream.

All of the laws produced by humanity have limits. God's perfect law—loving God with all our heart, and loving others as ourselves—has no inherent limit. We may effectually limit love by our attitudes, but otherwise, it is limitless.

God's commandment is perfect. God's law is complete and without limits for any need which we may have. It is relevant to any and every situation; it will never be outdated; it is eternal, reaching through all ages to all humanity. God's law can never be duplicated; it can never be fully comprehended. It is fulfilled in Christ, it is made manifest to us through the Holy Spirit. Following God's law will bring us wisdom, life, peace, and all the fullness of the Godhead.

3. Enemies — Verse 98

Your commandment makes me wiser than my enemies, (. . .). **TEV***: Your commandment (. . .) makes me wiser than my enemies.*

Jesus teaches us to love our enemies, and to pray for those who persecute us. This is not a concept the Psalmist knew, and he actually prayed curses on his enemies. In truth, all those who do not love the Lord or the Lord's commandments are the enemies of the Lord and the Lord's commandments. Obedience is the enemy of disobedience.

The Psalmist made many references to enemies: He expressed "hot indignation" because of those who forsook the Lord's law, in verse 53. In verse 139, his anger burned like a fire because his enemies disregarded the Lord's commands. According to verse 155, the wicked will not be saved because they are disobedient.

According to verse 61, feeling that the wicked had laid a trap for him, the Psalmist vowed loyalty to the Lord's law. The idea of a trap is also expressed in verse 110, but it would not cause disobedience. The Psalmist vowed meditation on the law, even though the wicked were trying to kill him, in verse 95.

In verse 84, the Psalmist was looking for the Lord to punish his persecutors. Verse 86 is interesting. First, the Psalmist spoke of the endurance or trustworthiness of the Lord's commandments. Then, he asked for help because of the persecution he endured. Does the persecution come because he follows trustworthy commandments? In verse 150, his persecutors drew nearer, and he described them as people who did not keep the Lord's law. Despite his many enemies and oppressors, the Psalmist, according to verse 157, would not fail to obey.

There is an inherent conflict in verse 113: Our author professed to hate those not completely loyal to the Lord, but to love the law of the Lord. If the Lord's law is love, this just can't work. A similar idea was expressed in verse 119. According to our Psalmist, God treats the wicked like rubbish, and so he loved God's instructions. Again, this goes against a law of love.

In verse 121, because he had done what is right and good, the Psalmist asked not to be abandoned to his enemies. Related to this is the unjust attack by powerful people of verse 161. Even though these attacks came, the Psalmist continued to respect the Lord's law.

It's not unusual that the Psalmist has enemies. Jesus had enemies. What the Psalmist seemed to miss is the concept of how the Lord can use enemies. As we saw in Christ's life, enemies can be used to fulfill God's purposes. Jesus was put to death, but that death was for the good of all creation, and came within God's plan. Jesus never called down curses on his enemies, and actually asked forgiveness for those who were putting him to death [Luke 23:34]. He never spoke of hating anyone. He obeyed the Father, and the purpose of the Father was fulfilled.

4. Evil — Verse 133

Keep my steps steady according to your promise, and never let iniquity have dominion over me. **TEV**: *As you have promised, don't let me be overcome by evil.*

These words come on a morning when—before my quiet time—I fixed coffee, sweet rolls, and bacon, on a weekday even. I guess I was thinking that was something pretty special. When the bacon—not cooked crisp—was criticized in an unpleasant way, I was hurt. I didn't holler, I stayed calm, but made some snide remarks. I felt, however, that evil had already won the day. I took my little breakfast into my quiet place, put on the armor, prayed Psalm 119:129–144, and found this passage.

The unpleasant little scene between my spouse and me could have been prevented. The Psalmist asked the Lord to prevent evil from controlling. It is good to ask that, but we have our parts also. God can prevent evil from overwhelming us; can stop the work of evil both from outside of us and from within, because Jesus has gained victory over evil. The Lord can keep me from doing evil and can keep others from overwhelming me with evil. We do have to submit to God, however, so he can do this work in our lives.

We have a choice to make. Will we be controlled by our flesh or by God's Spirit? That is one way God prevents evil from overwhelming us: by helping us make the right choices. Nothing is going to happen to me that God does not cause or allow. If it comes into my life, I have the promise that God will work through it for good in my life because I love him [Romans 8:28].

Evil is in the spiritual realm, so my spirit is what can be overwhelmed. We do not battle with flesh and blood [Ephesians 6:12]. It is my flesh, not my spirit, which responds in unkind ways. We have to learn to let the Spirit of God control our spirits, so that our spirits can control our flesh. It is not easy, but neither is it impossible.

We are composite beings: we are *spirit*, desiring—and often succeeding—to please God, trying to submit to God's Spirit. We are *bodies of flesh*, with sin ingrained like fat marbled through a good steak. It benefits the steak, but it doesn't benefit us. We have to melt it out, because the flesh is always opposed to God's ways. The flesh is very strong, but it does not have to prevail.

Besides the spirit and flesh, we are also made up of *soul*. This is a nebulous part of my being which is often used interchangeably with the spirit. There is a difference. My soul is who I am. It contains all my memories and experiences. These memories, remembering when I have succeeded and when I have failed to please God, can influence my responses, and so my soul also needs to be submitted to God's control.

What does it mean for us to be overcome? It means that we are defeated, encased. The overcoming factor controls and causes us to lose control. We forget our resources; we are robbed of strength; we are in the power of that which has overcome; we lose our identity; we are wiped out; swept away; stomped on—envision an ant hill; shaken; unable to stand; drowned; suffocated. Now, a lot of those things I would be willing to endure if it were God's Spirit that was overcoming me. No person desiring to serve the Lord can endure evil doing that to them.

Evil came into the world through the decision of two people to follow their own ways and ignore God's way. As I understand it, it manifests itself in two ways in our lives: from outside of us, and from within. From within, it is our flesh nature asserting itself, and from outside, it is the work of the forces of evil upon our lives. The two, of course, love to join forces. If I have a tendency to be drawn to particular sin, the enemy will see that the temptation for that sin is often put in my way.

From within, my flesh nature will try to promote bad things, making them seem desirable. Maybe they are things I enjoyed in my life before Christ. When I take my eyes off the Lord, many things will have appeal that would be rejected if my focus was in the right place. Some attitudes and characteristics that might try to assert themselves are: weakness in faith; self-control; lust; selfishness; jealousy; resentment; self-promotion; self-seeking; lying; and feelings of superiority. When these things cannot be quickly dealt with as soon as they appear, I know my flesh is in control.

Evil from outside of us can overwhelm us also. In addition to the enemy's use of our own weaknesses, the enemy can use evil inclinations of other people to overwhelm us. Bad influences can lead us astray. The enemy can also use the natural attitudes of others to hurt us. People may be indifferent to us; they may try to exalt themselves over us; they may not like us and they may even have the desire to hurt us. Besides the actual harm that others might do us, we might, in our own weaknesses, be overwhelmed by their negative attitudes toward us. It is really hard to always remember that if God is for us, anything anyone might do against us can have no effect that God does not desire.

The Psalmist dealt with evil or iniquity throughout his life. In his desire to be obedient, he declared that he had kept himself from every evil way, in verse 101. In verse 115, he commanded evildoers to flee from him, because they kept him from obeying the Lord's commandments. The Psalmist knew the powerful influence of the people who surrounded him. He recognized the evil purposes of some who drew near him, in verse 150, and knew that those who pursue such evil were not following God. The Psalmist also knew defeat, according to verse 25. As we read his words, we can only assume that this sense of defeat lasted only briefly, but he was, for a season, struck down by his enemies and sought God's hand to lift him.

VI
APPENDIX A

Verses Not Used in Focus or Reference:
Verses 2–5; 20, 22, 31, 39, 58, 68, 94, 105, 126, 170, 171, and 175.

As I consider the verses which I did not focus on devotionally or use as a reference, there is one that shouts for attention: Verse 105: *Your word is a lamp to my feet and a light to my path.* To me, that is what the whole Psalm is about: God's word guiding our lives. Each day, as I don the armor, I take up the Sword of the Spirit, which is the word of God [Ephesians 6:17]. I try to find Scripture that goes with each piece of armor, and verse 105, along with verse 11, go with the sword.

When we have the Light of the World within us, it should guide our paths, helping us to avoid missing the mark, which is sin. Scripture that is not studied can be of no help to us, but we have to go beyond reading. Hiding it in our hearts even goes beyond memorization. Memorization starts in the head. We have to bring it down to our hearts. We have to assimilate the words into our lives. Many people can quote words. More is required.

First, we must make sure we understand the words. This can be done by reading several versions of Scripture and by using aids such as Bible dictionaries, commentaries, and en-cyclopedias. It is important to get a variety of different views, and then bring them together to find an idea that is supported with other Scriptures. No Scripture stands alone in meaning.

Secondly, we have to make the words real to our lives. We can't talk about love if we do not love. Witnessing to others is useless if there is no love behind it. Whatever we preach, teach, or discuss in our lives must be something we are living. Since we aren't perfect, it's okay to say that something we are sharing is also something we are working on in our own lives. We just have to make sure we are making a serious and sincere effort.

VII
APPENDIX B

Alphabetic Hebrew Letters at the Beginning of Each Paragraph

Verse 1 — aleph: *ashray* — Happy. These eight verses talk about the blessing given to those who follow the way of the Lord.

Verse 9 — bet: *bamay* — In what, how. These verses discuss how one keeps his or her life pleasing to the Lord: by obeying, praising, repeating, delighting, studying, and taking pleasure in the way of the Lord.

Verse 17 — gimel: *g'mol* — deal with, recompense. These verses talk about the way the Lord rewards those who follow him, and responds to those who disobey.

Verse 25 — daleth: *davkah* — it clings, sticks (the soul to the dust). The Psalmist discusses defeat, and pleads for God's response to this.

Verse 33 — he: *'orayni* — teach me. The Psalmist looks for understanding by expressing such pleas as explain, keep me obedient, give me desire, save me, and give me new life.

Verse 41 — vav: *vivoaynee* — let come to me (your steadfast love). These verses discuss activities of the Psalmist because of God's love.

Verse 49 — zayin: *zecor-devar* — remember the word.

The Psalmist asks the Lord to remember his promise and discusses the results in his life of that promise.

Verse 57 — heth: *chelki* — my share or portion. The Psalmist discusses the sufficiency of the Lord in his life.

Verse 65 — teth: *tov* — good (noun). The Psalmist describes several ways in which the Lord has brought goodness into his life.

Verse 73 — yodh: *yadekah* — your hands. The hands which created the Psalmist will also bring justice and preservation.

Verse 81 — kaph: *koltah* — it languishes, faints, fails (the Psalmist's soul, for the Lord's salvation). The Psalmist discusses his despair as he waits for the Lord to act.

Verse 89 — lamedh: *l'olam* — forever. The Psalmist discusses the eternal character of the Lord's word and work.

Verse 97 — mem: *mah-ahavti* — what; (how) I love. The Psalmist discusses the benefits of and the ways he demonstrates his love for the law of the Lord.

Verse 105 — nun: *ner-l'ragli* — a lamp to my feet. The law of the Lord has brought joy and salvation in times of darkness.

Verse 113 — samekh: *se'phim* — the divided or half-hearted. The safety of those who trust in the Lord, compared to those who do not.

Verse 121 — ayin: *ashiti* – I do, have done. The Psalmist declares his obedience and claims the blessing of the Lord because of this.

Verse 129 — pe: *pe'laote* — wonders. A noun used as an adjective, as in (your teachings) are wonderful. The Psalmist discusses his desire to obey the wonderful teachings of the Lord.

Verse 137 — tsadhe: *tsadik* — righteous. The Psalmist discusses the righteousness and fairness of the Lord and His laws.

Verse 145 — qoph: *qaratie* — I call. These verses discuss times the Psalmist called upon the Lord, and asked the Lord to hear him.

Verse 153 — resh: *r'eh-onie* — look at my affliction. These verses voice the Psalmist's plea for help, based on the Lord's compassion and mercy.

Verse 161 — shin: *sharim* — princes. The Psalmist discusses some of the persecution he faces, and the steadfastness of the Lord in helping him.

Verse 169 — tav: *tiqrav* — let come near (my cry). The Psalmist pleads that the Lord will always be alert to his cry.

(Endnotes)

1   Ortberg, John. "God is Closer Than You Think," Zondervan, p. 15.

2   Donne, John, quoted in "Illustrations Unlimited," James Hewett, ed., Tyndale, p. 170.

3   Green, Michael, ed., "1500 Illustrations for Biblical Teaching," p. 295.

4   Barnhouse, Donald Grey. "Timeless Illustrations for Preaching and Teaching," Hendrickson, p. 247.

5   Allen, J. Timothy, "Seasons In The Year," Smyth and Helwys, p. 123.

6   Author/Editor unknown, "God's Little Devotional Book," Honor Books. p. 257.